Carbon Shinai
カーボンシナイ

- CF-Type
- DB-Type
- K1-Type
- K2-Type

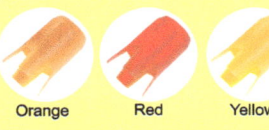

Orange　Red　Yellow

We have improved the official Carbon Shinai rubber stopper.

The NEW official rubber stopper.
¥300 (domestic Japanese price)

WARNING!!
Never use anything other than our official rubber stopper on your Carbon Shinai !!

When using your Carbon Shinai.....

1. To prevent injury, please use our official rubber stopper. Do not use stoppers made for conventional bamboo shinai on your Carbon Shinai, as there is a risk of injury to your opponent if the tip breaks through and enters their men grill.

2. When choosing a sakigawa (leather tip), make sure that it is more than 5cm in length and completely covers our rubber stopper. If the sakigawa is shorter than 5cm, there is a risk of injury to your opponent if a slat slips out and enters their men grill.

3. Do not shave the plastic surface of your Carbon Shinai. If you shave the surface, the black carbon fiber will be exposed, causing damage that may result in injury to your opponent.

4. Always check the condition of the surface of your Carbon Shinai before and during use. As soon as you notice any cracks, or peeling of the surface, or if black carbon fiber is exposed on any part of the outside, inside or edges of the Shinai, or you notice any other damage, stop using the shinai immediately. There is a danger of injury to your opponent if your Carbon Shinai is split or broken.

5. When tying the nakayui (leather binding), either tie a knot in the tsuru-ito (cord), or tie one end of the nakayui to the tsuru-ito, or by another means ensuring that is does not move up and down during use. If there is any damage whatsoever to the sakigawa, tsukagawa (hilt), rubber stopper, tsuru-ito and so on, replace them immediately.

6. If the tip of the Carbon Shinai is damaged, or a slat is protuding out of the sakigawa, there is a danger that it could enter your opponent's men grill and injure them.

Kendogu Revolution

Mu-Jun Men
武楯面

SG-Type

WARNING!!

1. Under no circumstances should organic solvents (such as thinner, alcohol, benzene, toluene, acetone, gasoline, kerosene, etc.), acidic or alkali chemicals, domestic cleansers, car cleansers, or anti-mist sprays, be used to clean the shield. These substances will cause the shield to deteriorate, leading to clouding, cracking or breaking, thereby resulting in danger of injury to the face.

2. Should the shield develop deep scratches or cracks on either the outer or inner surface, discontinue use of the shield immediately, and replace it with an undamaged shield. If the shield is used in such a condition, there is a danger of it breaking, causing injury to the face.

3. It should be fully understood that, as with the traditional Japanese Kendo-Men (mask), there is still the danger of injury to the face through fragments of broken bamboo or Carbon Shinai pieces penetrating through areas not covered by the shield.

- SCIENCE TO SEEK SAFETY -

HASEGAWA
HASEGAWA CORPORATION

WEB : http://kendo.hasegawakagaku.co.jp/
Email : contact@hasegawakagaku.co.jp

Carbon Shinai — Points to be checked

DANGER !! — Before these happen..... **ATTENTION !!**

Although the Carbon Shinai is much more durable than a conventional bamboo one, it will inevitably become damaged since it is a sword that is used to repeatedly strike and thrust your opponent. Therefore, inspect the condition of the surface, sides or reverse of the Carbon Shinai's slats before, during and after use, and stop using it immediately should damage like in the following pictures be observed. (These pictures are just a few examples of many.)

- Damage on the surface

- An unglued surface sheet

- Exposure of the Carbon fiber

- Longitudinal crack on the surface

- Damage and ungluing of the surface

- Crack on the reverse

There is the case where the reverse gets cracked even without any damage on the surface. Inspect the inside of the Shinai by pushing the pieces with the fingers and unbinding the Naka-yui.

HASEGAWA-KOTE

- Detachable and washable "Tenouchi" is easy to wash and dry.
- "Tenouchi" is replaceable when torn. No need to repair.

Tenouchi (Inner) — *Kote (Main part)*

- SCIENCE TO SEEK SAFETY -

HASEGAWA CORPORATION
http://kendo.hasegawakagaku.co.jp/

KENDO WORLD Volume 7.3   December 2014   Contents

Editorial	2
The 62nd All Japan Kendo Championships **A Changing of the Guard?**	4
The Nippon Budokan's 50th Anniversary	8
Grading Successfully: Part 3 Shigematsu Kimiaki (Kyoshi 8-dan)	10
Kendo for Adults	15
Passing 7-dan: Reflections after the Facts	18
Reidan-jichi Part 18 **Waza Basics**	20
Japanese School Kendo and My Journey from Yokohama to the U.S.	23
sWords of Wisdom **"Jūbun no make wa Jūbun no kachi"**	28
Historical Sightseeing **Owari Province**	30
Empty Mind Films: An Interview with Martial Arts Documentary Filmmaker **Jon Braeley**	34
45th Anniversary of Kendo in Buenos Aires, Argentina	41
Bujutsu Jargon Part 6	44
Review: **Kendo Playing Cards**	46
The 7th U.S. Nitō Kendo Camp	48
'A Man of Many Parts' Portrait of an Inimitable Swordsman	52
Lidstone Kyūsha Memorial Taikai	58
World Kendo Network	60
A Stranger in [Kendo] Paradise	62
Forsaken Kendo Katate guntō-jutsu	66
Musō Jikiden Eishin-ryū Riai The Meaning of the Kata: Part 1	74
The Great Hagakure Paradox —An Affirmation of Life?	82
Shinai Sagas **Always Armed**	84
Sports-related injuries in Kendo —a systematic review of the medical literature—	89

Kendo World Staff
- Bunkasha International President & Editor-in-Chief— Alex Bennett PhD
- Bunkasha International Vice President & Assistant Editor— Michael Ishimatsu-Prime MA
- Bunkasha International Vice President & Graphic Design— Shishikura 'Kan' Masashi
- Bunkasha International Vice President— Hamish Robison
- Bunkasha International Vice President— Michael Komoto MA
- Bunkasha International General Manager— Baptiste Tavernier MA
- Senior Consultants— Yonemoto Masayuki, Shima Masahiko

KW Staff Writers | Translators | Photographers | Graphic Designer | Sub-editors

Axel Pilgrim PhD	Jeff Broderick	Steven Harwood MA
Blake Bennett MA	Kate Sylvester MA	Stuart Gibson
Bruce Flanagan MA	Lockie Jackson PhD	Taylor Winter
Bryan Peterson	Miho Maki	Tony Cundy
Charlie Kondek	Paul Benson	Trevor Jones
Gabriel Weitzner	Scott Huegel (MaSC)	Tyler Rothmar
Honda Sōtarō PhD	Sergio Boffa PhD	Yamaguchi Remi
Imafuji Masahiro MBA	Stephen Nagy PhD	Vivian Yung

KW would like to thank the following people and organisations for their valuable cooperation:
- All Japan Kendo Federation
- All Japan Budogu
- Hasegawa Teiichi - President, Hasegawa Corporation
- *Kendo Jidai* Magazine
- *Kendo Nihon* Magazine
- Nippon Budokan Foundation
- Shogun Kendogu
- TOZANDO

Guest Writers
- Alan Stephenson (Junshinkan Kendo Club, NZ)
- Alexander Thomas (Lidstone Taikai participant)
- Daryl Tong, (Assoc. Prof. Otago University)
- Donatella Castelli (Kendo Renshi 7-dan, World Kendo Network)
- Hatano Toshio (Kendo Kyōshi 8-dan,
- Kim Taylor (Iaido 7-dan, sdksupplies.com)
- Ōya Minoru (Prof. International Budo University; Kendo Kyōshi 7-dan)
- Paul Budden (Kendo Kyōshi 7-dan, Kodokan Kendo U.K.)
- Robert Stroud (Kendo Kyōshi 7-dan, Idaho Kendo Club)
- Shigematsu Kimiaki (Kendo Kyōshi 8-dan)
- Tabata Ko (Southeast Missouri State University)

COPYRIGHT 2014 Bunkasha International Corporation. No part of this publication may be reproduced in any form whatsoever without written permission from the publisher, except by writers who are permitted to quote brief passages for the purpose of review or reference. Kindly contact Bunkasha International Corporation at info@kendo-world.com.

Editorial Conventions Used in KW Inevitably in a magazine of this nature, many non-English words appear in the text. All Japanese words are italicised and include macrons (ū, ō) etc., apart from common place names and nouns, and words in some captions and headings. As a general exception, KW treats all the martial arts (budo), such as kendo, iaido, jodo, ranks, and so on as Anglicised words without using macrons. Japanese names are written in accordance to the traditional Japanese manner of family name followed by given name. Traditional *ryūha* are written with capitals and therefore are not italicised. 'Kata' with a capital 'K' refers to the set of Nippon Kendo Kata, and *kata* refers to set forms in general. The masculine personal pronoun is used throughout the text in some articles in the interest of readability, and is in no way meant to slight the significant contributions made by female kendoka.

Editorial Alex Bennett
No Riff-raff Please!

An interesting fact: the word "boo" was first bawled in the early 19th century to replicate the sound that cows make. Now of course, Bovinese is attempted with the more onomatopoeically precise "moo". Later on in the 19th century, however, "boo" became the favoured expression for those who would condemn. Incidentally, its predecessor, "hoot", was apparently hollered as early as 1225 as a sign of derision or contempt. But, who gives two hoots anyway? What has this got to do with our beloved art of kendo?

Given that the 16WKC is just around the corner, I thought it might be timely to revisit spectator etiquette. Especially as this topic received a considerable thrashing on the internet and in Japanese kendo magazines after the 15WKC held in Novara, 2012. Those who were there will remember some rather awkward moments in the final for the men's teams—Japan versus Korea. The *shinpan* made their calls, the Korean *senshu* glared at them in disbelief, certain elements of the crowd enunciated their dissonance towards a) *shinpan*, or, b) *senshu*; and many more enunciated their dissonance at the enunciations of dissonance. The result was a confused cacophony of booing and hissing, bolstered by lashings of hooting—an unruly commotion that has no place at a kendo tournament.

In most sports, spectators can pretty much yell and bawl all they like. Barring sanctionable offences such as racist comments, supporter decorum is relatively loose, and pugnacious heckling is the accepted norm these days. Booing the opposition and/or the umpire when things don't go your team's way makes the sporting venue an emotional hothouse for insulting banter, profanity, and unashamed flaunting of the most crude, uncivilised elements of humanity. Sad though it is, this infusion of 'passion' (sometimes fuelled by alcohol) intensifies the excitement; and I must confess to being culpable in this regard when the All Blacks—New Zealand's national rugby team—are putting their opponents to the sword.

Even "streakers" are commonplace these days—at least in international rugby and cricket back in my old country—although it is difficult to tell if the crowd is cheering or jeering in most cases. The inevitable ferocious tackle of the brazen naked perpetrator by overzealous security guards will elicit a 60,000-strong collective groan as the crowd cringes at the painful crunch, followed by roars of excited laughter; akin, I would hazard a guess, to the rumpus ensuing the gladiator's *coup de grace* in ancient Rome. There's not much respect there, just a crass mob mentality driven by the thirst for gore.

Some sports, however, are very strict with crowd behaviour. At golf tournaments, you risk expulsion from the gallery for a poorly timed cough. It is considered jolly bad form to taunt tennis players at Wimbledon, a venue and event which prides itself on exemplary sportsmanship. It is reprehensible, for example, to rejoice a double fault or poor shot. The organisers even promulgated a strict dress and attitude code for spectators in addition to the already long-establish players' uniform protocols. Their actual words were: "No riff-raff please, we're Wimbledon".

One would expect budo to have the same kind of rules given the emphasis placed on respect and propriety. Recently, I had the sports channel on in the background, and the clamour of excited fans blared from the speakers. Without actually looking at the TV, I assumed that an English Premiere League football match had just got under way. When I realised that it was not soccer but "Grand Slam Judo Tokyo" (formerly Jigoro Kano Cup Tokyo International Judo Tournament) on the box, I could hardly believe my eyes, and ears…

The fact that tournament is now called "Grand Slam" and cash prizes are awarded is curious enough, but such is the world of judo now. Top level judo athletes need to travel and compete successfully to accrue points to qualify for the Olympics. Those who stand on the Olympic podium have pretty much achieved the ultimate goal in judo today; but they need prize money and sponsorship to get there. The commercialisation of budo is a topic I will leave for another time. Suffice it to say, Jigoro Kano's original educational ideals of respect and using one's strengths for the greater good are now ostensibly little more than secondary considerations after collecting gold medals.

Notwithstanding this aspect of competitive judo, it was the vociferous spectators and their loud incantations that bemused me. I am not saying that the spectators were badly behaved as far as big sports events go, nor was there a lot of booing or catcalling. But is effusive cheering acceptable in a budo competition? Quite frankly, I don't think so.

With regards to kendo, we are taught that respect for our opponents is of paramount importance given the overtly violent nature of what we are doing. We are told to be modest in victory and gracious in defeat. We should never argue with the *shinpan*, irrespective of whether or not their judgements are correct. We are tutored that both winning and losing provides us with clues for developing our kendo, and by extension, our character. Watching the *keiko* or *shiai* of others (*mitori-geiko*) is also a useful means for improvement, so spectating at a tournament is actually a part of our training rather than entertainment.

As such, tournaments are a formal occasion for study, not revelry. Let's take a leaf out Wimbledon's book and dress appropriately for the occasion. Let's politely clap a successful result with a mode of decorum and propriety, if there is to be any clapping at all. No cheering *hansoku*, please! And, just as competitors will have an *ippon* rescinded if they insult their opponent or let rip with a victory pose, the kendoka in the crowd should surely demonstrate the same self-control, sincerity, and polite manner.

Alas, in Japan I have frequently been witness to cheers of exuberance with the awarding of *hansoku*, and coordinated jeers of 'disapproval' or 'disbelief' to put pressure on the *shinpan* from the safety of the bleachers. Many people also make known their dismay when their team loses the match. Why not be glad to witness a stonking *ippon*, regardless of who the striker is? Of course, nobody WANTS to lose, but isn't the right budo attitude to "keep calm and carry on"—not "carrying on"—once the bout is decided? Then there are those who just up and leave once their team has been eliminated, instead of staying to learn a thing or two from the winning teams. Unforgiveable though, are those who just leave their rubbish where they were sitting. This is such a problem in Japan, that students are actually finding it difficult to secure venues for their tournaments!

This is not even a matter of spectator etiquette, but more one of common sense. From a kendo perspective though, the way you watch a match is a good indication of your understanding of kendo values. It behooves all of us to keep these things in mind at the 16WKC, and any other tournament. No riff-raff please, we're kendo.

Have a great 2015, and we hope to see you in Tokyo for the 16WKC.

62nd All Japan Champion, Takenouchi Yūya

THE 62ⁿᴰ ALL JAPAN KENDO CHAMPIONSHIPS
A Changing of the Guard?

By Michael Ishimatsu-Prime

In my report in Kendo World 7.1 on the AJKC last year, I wrote about how it would be remembered for Uchimura Ryōichi's continued dominance as he sealed his third title while not conceding a point and needing enchō to win only twice. I also noted the emergence of Hokkaido's Ando Shō who made it to the semi-final in only his second outing. However, this year's edition will be remembered for an entirely different reason; for this was the year when, in front of a crowd of 8,761 at the Nippon Budokan, Japan's youth stamped their authority on the AJKC and signalled a probable changing of the guard. The new champion, Takenouchi Yūya, a 21-year-old third-year university student, was at the vanguard.

With the possible exception of Tokyo's Takahashi Hideto, who made it to the quarter-final stage, as well as defeated semi-finalist Hatakenaka Kōsuke (Tokyo), the big names failed to shine this year. Coming off the back of taking the Police Individual Competition title a week before, Hatakenaka was clinical throughout the tournament, and he will no doubt feel aggrieved at losing to Takenouchi in the semi-final. Kotani Akinori (Chiba), last year's runner-up, went out in the first round, as did Hokkaido's Andō Shō, who placed third last year. Tokyo's Shōdai Masahiro, also third last year, lost in the second round like Osaka's Furukawa Kōsuke, who has a third-place finish on his resume, not to mention victories in the WKC (team) and Police Team Competition. The two highest ranked (R7-dan) and oldest (38) kenshi, Saitama's Yoneya Yūichi and Kanagawa's Hōjō Tadaomi, fell in the second round against much more youthful opposition. Then there was defending champion Uchimura Ryōichi who lost in the third round to Oita's Takeshita Yōhei (26). Experience counts for a lot in kendo, something that we can all attest to having been toyed with by sensei in their 70s and 80s, but that seemed not to be the case at this AJKC.

Kunitomo (L) vs. Takenouchi (R) in the final

To say that the young competitors in the AJKC are "inexperienced" is not correct as they have most likely been fed on a diet of shiai throughout their high school and university years. It is a big step up, however, to the AJKC. In recent years a few students have qualified for the AJKC, but have not progressed far. The most notable exception to this is Hatakenaka Kōsuke, who, as a fourth-year Kokushikan University student, achieved a best-eight finish. This year there were four students in the finals. The University of Tsukuba had two: Takenouchi representing Fukuoka, and Kawai Ryōsuke (23, Ibaraki), a postgraduate student. There was also Yamada Yūki (22, Nara), a fourth-year from Osaka's Kansai University, and Asada Hiroki (21, Tottori), a third-year from International Pacific University in Okayama.

Yamada lost in the first round against Shimada Takafumi (31, 5-dan, Saitama) but competed admirably against his older and more experienced opponent. Asada won his first round encounter against Kamamura Naoya (34, R6-dan, Ehime) but was then defeated by the above-mentioned Takahashi. Kawai beat Osaka's Tomoi Kōichirō (34, R6-dan) in the first round, but was then undone in a great second-round encounter by his Tsukuba kohai and eventual winner, Takenouchi Yūya.

Takeshita (R) launches a tsuki against Kunitomo in the QF

Takenouchi was a revelation at this AJKC. K8-dan Shigematsu Kimiaki-sensei, match analyst for Kendo World, commented that he was calm beyond his years, not allowing the connection between him and his opponent to be broken during his matches making him very difficult to fight against. He also had many tricks up his sleeve. It was well known before the tournament that Takenouchi was something special. He was a well-known high school competitor, and had won the junior individual title at the 2013 Combat Games in Russia. The University of Tsukuba thinks so much of him that they want to keep him there after graduation to teach future students. Probably all of the nation's police forces would like him to join their tokuren teams.

At 21 years and 5 months, Takenouchi is the youngest ever winner of the AJKC, but he is not the only 21-year-old to have been crowned champion: company worker Kuwahara Tetsuaki was 21 years and 9 months (8th AJKC, 1960); Kawazoe Tetsuo was 21 years and 10 months (19th AJKC, 1971) and a fourth-year at Kokushikan University.

Like Kuwahara and Kawazoe, Takenouchi won the AJKC in his debut. Before Kuwahara in 1960, six of the seven titles were also won by debutants, but the AJKC was a fledgling competition then, so that was to be expected. Since Kuwahara, however, there have been several: Chiba Masashi (22, 14th AJKC, 1966), the aforementioned Kawazoe, Yokoo Eiji (24, 22nd AJKC, 1974), Migita Kōjirō (23, 24th AJKC, 1976), Ishibashi Masahisa (27, 26th AJKC, 1978) and Miyazaki Masahiro (27, 38th AJKC, 1990). Takenouchi was therefore the first person in 24 years to win in his debut competition.

Before Takenouchi, the last person to make it to the final on their debut was Tokyo's Harada Satoru in 1996, who was 23 at the time. He was eventually defeated by Miyazaki Masahiro in the final, in what became his fourth title. But, let us not forget that both finalists this year, Takenouchi, and 24-year-old policeman Kunitomo Rentarō, also from Fukuoka, were in their first AJKC. If Kunitomo had won, he would have been the seventh or eighth youngest champion, but this was not the youngest ever final. That was in 1971 between Kawazoe and Sayama Haruo, 23.

This year, three of the four semi-finalists were in their first competition, the other being Nishimura Hidehisa (25, 5-dan, Kumamoto), a former student individual champion and Todōfuken winner. In fact, this is the first time since 1976 that the final four have all been in their twenties.

Historically, the AJKC is a competition that favours older competitors, but this year was clearly quite different. Of the 62 champions to date, 40 have been 30 or over when winning their title, 55 when 25 or over. The average age of AJKC champions before this tournament was 31 years and 4 months – Takenouchi is ten years younger than that. Miyazaki Mashiro, who dominated the AJKC throughout the 1990s winning six titles, was 27 when he won his first title; Uchimura, 26. In fact, since 1990 when Miyazaki won his first title, only five champions have been in their twenties.

Another astonishing fact about Takenouchi's victory was the amount of time he was actually competing. Of the four semi-finalists, only Nishimura, at 23m15s, had spent less time on the shiai-jō in the previous four rounds than Takenouchi, who had been on for 24m33s. When Hatakenaka faced Takenouchi in the quarter-final, he had been fighting for a total of 43m32, almost double the time than that of Takenouchi. Then in the final, Takenouchi had fought for 25m41s compared to Kunitomo's 57m19s. Takenouchi had spent less than half of the time in the shiai-jō than Kunitomo by the final. As Takenouchi had beaten Hatakenaka in 1m08s in the semi-final compared to Kunitomo's 13m50s semi-final, Takenouchi was obviously fresher than his opponent.

As you can see, Takenouchi's victory was undoubtedly special, but here are some more interesting points of trivia about his victory.

Only two of Takenouchi's matches went into enchō, and of the remaining four, all but one were settled by two ippon.

He only conceded one ippon, and that was in the second round against his sempai from the University of Tsukuba, Kawai Ryōsuke.

On his way to the title, Takenouchi scored 10 ippon, seven of which were men, the others being two dō and one kote. Takenouchi was the first winner from Fukuoka since 1978; this was the first ever final with two Fukuoka representatives.

Takenouchi was the first non-police officer to win the AJKC since Hayashi Akira, a Hokkaido Kendo Federation staff worker, in 1988. In the history of the AJKC, only 17 winners have not been policemen.

It is going to be interesting to see where Takenouchi goes from here as he is still only a third-year student at college. What this tournament has shown us is that the future of Japanese kendo appears to be filled with promise. Pedigree competitors such as Nishimura and Takeshita will almost certainly be back, as will runner-up Kunitomo and his fantastic men strike. Then there is Hatakenaka who will no doubt bounce back after his semi-final defeat, as will Andō. The fact that four students qualified this year shows that there are many young kendoka with considerable talent out there. The AJKC will surely be just as exciting next year.

Nishimura (R) goes for Takahashi's kote in the QF

THE NIPPON BUDOKAN'S 50TH ANNIVERSARY

By Bryan Peterson

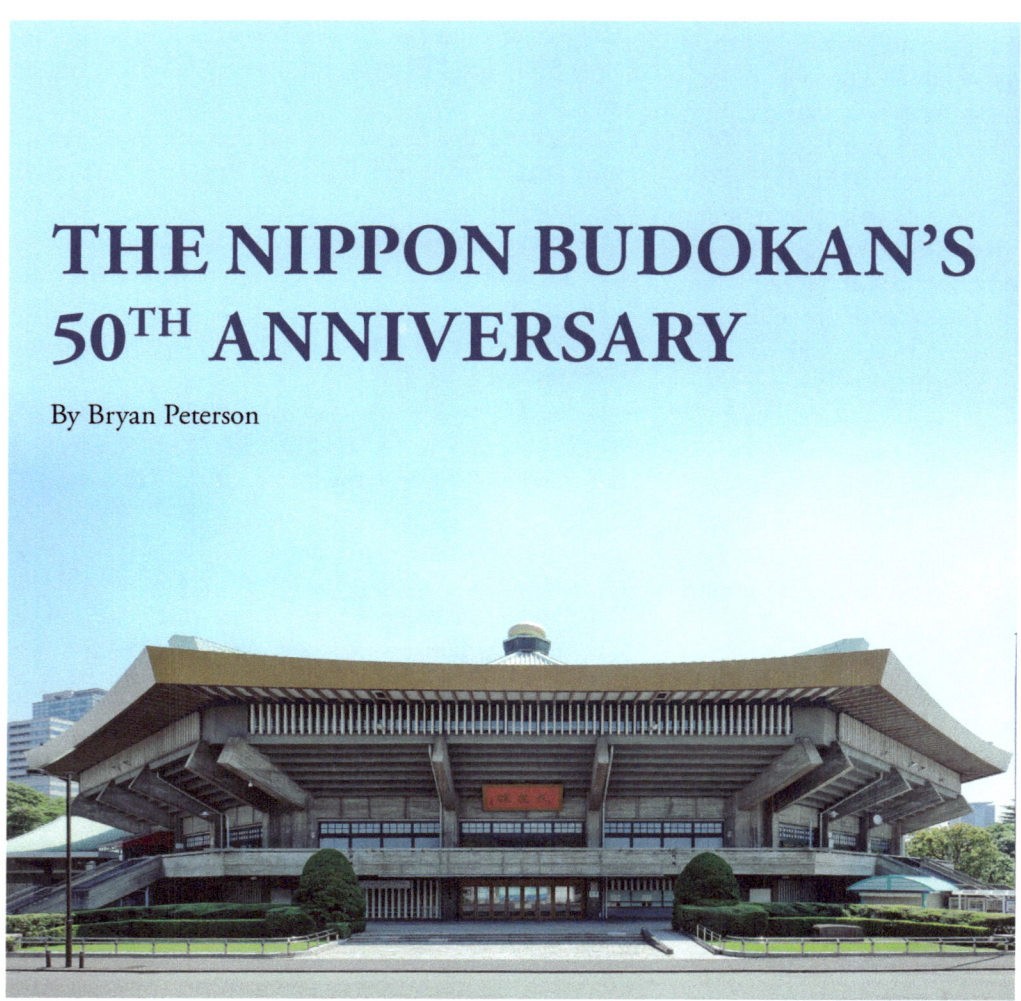

This year Nippon Budokan is celebrating its 50th anniversary. Many Japanese people remember 1964 as the year that Tokyo hosted the Olympics – an event which signified Japan's recovery from poverty and destruction in the wake of the Second World War.

The Nippon Budokan has played a key role in the preservation and dissemination of Japanese martial ways since its completion in 1964. The formal opening was held on October 3, followed by demonstrations of kendo, kyudo, and sumo on October 15. Nippon Budokan then served as the site for the judo competition in the 1964 Tokyo Olympics, from October 20-23. It was at this event that Dutch judoka Anton Geesink famously won a gold medal in the Open Weight Division.

Below are some key events at the Nippon Budokan from the past half-century:

1965: First *kagami-biraki*
1968: Inauguration of the Japanese Academy of Budo, an organisation which conducts academic research into the history and practice of budo.
1971: Inception of the Nippon Budokan Research Centre, a place which hosts events for scholars and martial artists.
1975: Launch of the *Budō Gekkan* magazine, a monthly publication covering various Japanese martial arts.
1976: Site of the Muhammad Ali vs. Antonio Inoki bout, seen as a predecessor of MMA matches.
1978: Dispatch of Japanese instructors overseas begins.
1979: Formation of the Japanese Association of Budo, an organization devoted to the preservation of older, traditional Japanese martial arts (*bujutsu*).
1984: International Budo University opens its doors.
1989: First annual International Seminar of Budo Culture.

Nippon Budokan also hosts the Budo Gakuen, offering numerous ongoing martial arts classes. In addition, there are many opportunities to take part in one-time demonstration lessons. Through such opportunities,

Japanese and non-Japanese alike can gainer further exposure to and knowledge of Japanese budo.

Many other events are hosted by Nippon Budokan, such as calligraphy competitions and annual national championships for several martial arts. It is also quite famous as a music venue.

The first concert there was held in 1966 when The Beatles played five consecutive nights. There was a bit of initial concern, as reported by the BBC: "Thirty-five thousand policemen guarded the group from their fans and from nationalist protestors who threatened to disrupt the concerts. They believed a foreign pop group would "desecrate" a hall which had been built for judo and other "noble" martial arts". [1]

The furore seems to have subsided over the years, and The Beatles have been followed by a steady stream of musical acts from around the world. Many famous live albums have been recorded at the Budokan, including those by Cheap Trick, Bob Dylan, Ozzy Osbourne, Santana, and Eric Clapton.

This year, Nippon Budokan is celebrating its long history of promoting budo with special events such as one held on October 5, 2014. Current Prime Minister Shinzō Abe spoke at the ceremony to commemorate its fiftieth anniversary.

Another milestone in Nippon Budokan history will be in 2020, when Tokyo will again host the Olympics. Quite fittingly, the judo competition is slated to be held there once again.

Before that, though, the Nippon Budokan will host the 16th World Kendo Championships in May 2015. See you there!

[1] Duncan Bartlett, BBC News 2008 (accessed Dec 6, 2014)

Photos courtesy of the Nippon Budokan Foundation

GRADING SUCCESSFULLY: Part 3

By Shigematsu Kimiaki, Kendo K8-dan
Translated by Remi Yamaguchi

"Cultivating your own kendo philosophy" (continued from Kendo World 7.2)

In this final instalment, Shigematsu-sensei continues his discussion on cultivating your own kendo philosophy and how it relates to success in grading as well as life outside of the dojo.

1. Disregarding strikes that fall below your ability

Whether it is a promotion exam or not, everybody knows what a perfect cut is. It is easy to say that you need to agitate your opponent to create an opening, and then strike immediately to get the *ippon*. This is, however, easier said than done, as the opponent is trying desperately to do the same. The difference lies in how you feel about *keiko*. You might complain, "Although I struck my opponent, they didn't acknowledge it as *ippon*." The same remarks would probably be directed towards referees in a match that was lost, or judges in a failed exam, but comments of this nature make you sound as if you are insisting on the validity of a strike.

Everybody strikes their opponent expecting it will be counted as *ippon*. This is subjective, not objective thinking. An *ippon* is something that convinces the opponent, as well as referees in a match, and examiners in a promotion examination. Furthermore, spectators also need to be convinced. Doing *keiko* with cuts that are only

99% is never going to be good enough. You need to strive for 100% in your regular *keiko*, otherwise you will end up complaining when your attempts are not acknowledged.

2. Seek and learn

There are various ways to commit oneself in *keiko* depending on the person, and their position and environment. Try always to have clear goals and be passionate about what you do. I imagine that everybody is sacrificing their work and family time to go to *keiko*. In spite of the sacrifice, you still need to take it up a notch and become even more proactive. If you engage in *keiko* with the same people at the same place all of the time, you will get too used to that environment, and you will lose the sense of tension that should always be present. It will become *keiko* for *keiko*'s sake.

You never know what style your opponent will have in exams or matches. This is why you should have a proactive attitude and try to "seek" new adversaries. If you have the opportunity, seek a new place to go and train in addition to your usual venue. This will help you to fight effectively against people with different styles, and your kendo will become more versatile. You will also be able to work on new problems that you encounter.

Another matter for consideration is aspiration for improvement. You must be willing to "learn". There are many learning opportunities such as seminars and training camps where you can gain useful knowledge. Practise what you learned, and see if it works for you. If it does, consider how you are going to "make it your own". This kind of experimentation will improve your kendo.

Unfortunately, there are some *kōdansha* who lack this learning attitude. Such people are called "*sensei*" by those around them, and they are actively "training" others. Their students are doing *keiko* and learning under their guidance, but are they working on improving their own kendo? If not, this constitutes a negligence.

Kendo training is a path that is tough and harsh, with no end in sight. Even though you may not see light at the end of the tunnel, maintaining a proactive attitude and seeking the light anyway as you aspire for improvement is the essence of kendo training. When you become good enough to be referred to as "*sensei*", you might find yourself wallowing in complacency. Be careful.

3. Keiko on your own

Through the medium of a *shinai*, you and your opponent teach each other about your flaws, and help improve each other's skills. *Hitori-geiko* (solitary *keiko*) is where you try to complement your own shortcomings remedially on your own. There are two kinds of *hitori-geiko*: where you train yourself to improve your skills, and where you try to improve your mental strength.

One of the typical exercises you can do to improve your skills is *suburi*, which is very effective for enhancing the sharpness of your *tenouchi* and the weight of your strikes. *Suburi* is not just indispensable for beginners, but for anyone who practises kendo. Also, many people learn some form of *koryū* (classical martial arts) alongside their regular kendo to introduce technical and mental elements into their training.

Something that can help mental strength is Zen meditation. Swordsmen of old enriched their mental strength through Zen, and disciplined themselves so that they could forge an "immoveable heart". Developing dignity and grace necessitates solitary training to keep your mind still. Being surprised and succumbing to fear are "movements of the mind". This is directly connected to your breathing, and if you become breathless in the course of offense and defence, it means that your mind is disturbed.

Breathing techniques are important to master, and currently the most popular style is a *tanden* (lower abdomen) breathing method, which requires considerable effort. You inhale quickly and exhale slowly for as long as possible using your abdominal muscles. You can develop your *tanden* this way, and also boost your *ki* (vital energy). By enhancing the *ki* in your *tanden*, you will not lose your breath so easily amid the fray. Then, you will become full of energy, and it will allow you to attack your opponent without hesitation. For this reason, some people even describe kendo's assailing process as an attempt to disturb each other's breathing.

When you are inhaling, you are in the state of *kyo* (not ready), and you are volatile. It is especially dangerous after you release *kiai*. You need to inhale so quickly that your opponent does not notice. On the contrary, when you are exhaling, this is the state of *jitsu* (ready), and you will be stable and replete with energy. Assail (*seme*) your opponent while exhaling. The *ki* you generate in your *tanden* will transfer to your left fist, then to your *shinai*, and will eventually manifest in the tip of your sword. You should strike as you exhale sharply. This breathing is critical in kendo. There is a saying that "breathing and *ki* are united". Strengthening your mind and forging *ki* also means developing your breathing.

I also recommend remedial physical training. When you are young, you are more dependent on your physical strength in *keiko*. As you get older, you will certainly notice a physical decline. Many people start to feel that

the strikes they used to manage from a certain interval (*maai*) gradually become impossible to pull off. *Ki* cannot be developed unless you are training yourself physically, as with the maxim "A sound mind in a sound body." By training your legs and hips, your ki will become more complete, and through being mentally settled, your *keiko* will become more robust. It is ideal to fortify the lower body so that you have the strength to endure *keiko*, and you can continue practising the basics. To this end, the benefits of *hitori-geiko* are immense.

4. Discipline your mind in your everyday life

Your kendo training is not confined to the dojo. Of course, the dojo is your main training venue, but it is possible to discipline your mind in your daily life. For example, going to *keiko* in the summer even though you know it will be very hard, or standing barefooted on the floor in the winter even though it is extremely cold. These are ways to train yourself though facing difficulty, rather than running away from it. Use your mornings in the same way. I am sure most people rely on an alarm clock to wake up. You should get up immediately instead of using the snooze function when the alarm goes off. This is like *sutemi*. When you think like this, and spring into action in daily life, this will be useful in *keiko*.

"*Zengo saidan*" is a teaching that means "Yesterday does not matter, neither does tomorrow. What matters is now, so live the moment." Cherishing every second, and every moment, helps to develop your *ki*. Whatever you do, it is all dependent on your level of motivation. If you are trying to foster your spirit, and yet decide to skip something that day, you will end up becoming a person devoid of real grit. In everything, the three *shin* (minds) are important: *hosshin* is motivation; *kesshin* is determination; *sōzokushin* is continuation.

H9-dan Ogawa Chūtarō-sensei said, "Do whatever task you've been given seriously. If you do that, your kendo ability will never wilt." Even if you have no time to go to the dojo, find a way of training yourself in the course of your everyday life. That way, you can discipline your mind, and rest assured that it will also help improve your kendo.

5. Instructor qualities

Kendo is a sublimated form of *kenjutsu*, which was created through the trials and tribulations of our predecessors. It is a traditional form of Japanese culture that has a long history and has been passed down from generation to generation. Instructors are responsible for inheriting the teachings and correctly conveying the knowledge to future generations. They need to teach "proper kendo", but what does that mean? It means the acquisition of technical mastery, and the cultivation of the mind.

The techniques have to be based on the principles underlying the method of using real swords. This necessitates paying attention to *hasuji* (blade angle) and *shinogi* (side of the blade) during *keiko*. When it comes to cultivation of the mind, it means to develop a sense of uprightness, humility, and manners. "Uprightness" means to act morally; "humility" to maintain integrity and have a sense of shame; "manners" refers to knowing how to behave appropriately around others.

Recently, people seem to have lost sight of such goals in kendo. They appear to be rather skill-oriented and too concerned about winning and losing. Why is this so? Perhaps it is because instructors feel strongly that unless their students achieve good results, their value as an instructor will diminish. There are teachings such as "*sossen suihan*" (to set an example worth following) and "*shihan dōgyō*" (students and teachers are on the same path). I believe that a good instructor should take the initiative in *keiko*, and understand what good, dignified kendo is. They must cultivate their own mind and become able to teach correct kendo without focusing only on the technical side of kendo.

6. Do your students appreciate your instruction?

It is hard to pass promotion exams. What is harder, however, is to do kendo that matches the grade you pass. When instructing your students, you need to make sure that you do not give them reason to say or think things like, "He talks the talk, but he ain't walking the walk."

There is a truism that says, "Vows made in storms are forgotten in the calm." I sometimes see people who, feeling bitter after many failed attempts, finally pass and then instantly become more critical, and do nothing but condemn flaws in others. I almost feel like pointing out that if they know so much, they should have passed much sooner.

If your grade becomes higher, you will have more opportunities to teach others. Make your kendo something that everybody looks up to, and they will seek your instruction to emulate your style of kendo. To instruct others is to convey your theory or your kendo philosophy. It has to be worthy of that privilege.

I took my first 8-dan grading in Tokyo in November 2006 when I was 47. I was full of confidence but the result was far from satisfactory. From then, I travelled between Kyoto and Tokyo for the examination, and finally, in Kyoto on May 1, 2009, I was fortunate enough to pass on my sixth attempt at the age of 50.

Since passing the grade of 8-dan, I pledged to carry out the following three things: First, I will keep my kendo strong when I am 60, 10 years after my promotion. This means not just having the ability to strike my opponent. Attacking my opponents with my *ki*, agitating them so that openings arise, and then seizing that opportunity and striking—this is the kind of kendo I want to keep working on. I do not attempt a strike unless I overwhelm my opponent with my *seme*. To do this, I need to keep developing my *ki*. The best way to enhance *ki* is to attack the opponent incessantly during *kakari-geiko*. Once you become 8-dan, however, there are fewer opportunities to do this as you are required to be *motodachi*. Therefore, I make it a rule to ask higher-level sensei to train me three times a month.

Second, I pledged to work on my physical condition so that I can continue to endure rigorous *keiko*. As I use trains, cars, and buses, I feel that my legs are getting weaker and my basic physical strength is declining as I get older. The less physical strength I have, the harder it will be to do kendo, which puts me at risk of injury. After becoming 8-dan, there are many times when you would have to be *motodachi* for an extended period of time. Without adequate physical strength, it is impossible to perform satisfactory *keiko*. As the body is fundamental to doing kendo, it is necessary to maintain core power, and strengthen the legs, back, and abdomen to avoid injury.

Third, I pledged to constantly reflect on my kendo. I failed the 8-dan grading five times. The fact that I failed means that my kendo did not meet the requirements of Article 14 of the "Regulations for Dan/Kyu and Shogo Title Certificates". Fortunately, I was able to receive instruction and advice from many sensei, which helped me pass on my sixth try. Right now I am trying to reflect on my past kendo failures and figure out what caused them. Everybody has flaws. *Shugyō* is to find your flaws, and to remedy them throughout your life. It is important to always self-examine, find your shortcomings, and try to fix them.

7. Kendo is about developing willpower

Ultimately, kendo depends on willpower. Your skills may improve as time passes, but your body will get weaker. Therefore, if you are too dependent on skills that require physical ability, you will eventually reach an impasse. To continue kendo for a long time, you need to seriously engage in *keiko* with the basics of kendo in mind. Kendo evokes words such as "tough" and "hard". When you

think about *shochū-geiko* in mid-summer, and *kan-geiko* when your feet go numb with cold, it seems so irrational. This is because *keiko* is not just about improving your skills; it is also about disciplining your mind. Bolstering your mental attitude and fortitude is the crucial objective of *shugyō*.

I had the pleasure of writing the dictum "*kensokushin*" on a *shinai* bag that was created as a commemorative gift for the 25th anniversary of the Shūdōkai kendo club. It means, "Through training, discipline your mind and apply it to your kendo". I believe that the main point of kendo is that the sword trains the mind, and the mind trains the sword.

Even if you do not perform well in *shiai* when you are young, by trying to work on the basics and building up your skills, you will eventually be able to develop more than those who do not. I think that in kendo "great talent matures later". There is no shortcut—stick to the basics and do *keiko* as often as possible. It is important that kendo does not just become the act of simple striking. Practise with determination and enough willpower to become a role model in everybody's eyes.

8. Keiko alone is not enough

To make your kendo stronger, do *keiko* as often as possible. Also, the content of your *keiko* needs to be well-planned and well-executed. Regardless of your age or grade, never neglect the basics – specifically, *kirikaeshi* and *uchikomi*. They are the fundamental exercises that you should never skip.

Still, you might wonder if just sticking to the basics is all you need to improve your kendo. I do not believe so. Indeed there are some people who can become strong just by doing *keiko*, but I think they are in the minority. Regular people like me cannot expect too much out of just doing *keiko*. You may experience some steady improvement in skill, but you will hit a wall sooner or later. What makes the difference is how you overcome that impasse. You should build up enough strength to overcome obstacles. Take the initiative and try to absorb anything that might help your kendo.

Personally, I go running as it trains my lower body. Mentally it makes me feel good. Furthermore, I practise breathing from my *tanden*. It is only for ten minutes every day, but it enriches my mind, makes me settled, and by extension, it also improves my *keiko*.

Those with true ability still make an effort in other areas. While they may appear to be doing only *keiko*, they are most likely engaging in extra-curricular activities. Realise that *keiko* alone will not fully expand your kendo—you need a little something extra, something to complement what you cannot achieve only through *keiko*.

9. Conclusion

I decided to pen this series of three articles to be of help to fellow kendo practitioners. I wrote about the kendo philosophy that I have cultivated through my own training, but due to my limited talent, I am afraid it is still rather shallow. I understand that people have different values, so some may agree with my ideas while others may not. I have no intention of forcing my *keiko* methods on anybody, but I hope that what I have written is of some help. Last but not least, I wish all of my fellow kendoka the best of luck along their journey.

The Keiko Mind-set

If your mind seeks a higher level of kendo, your keiko will change.
If your keiko changes, your lifestyle will change.
If your lifestyle changes, your values for kendo will change.
As your kendo values change, you will find your own way.
Do not look up, do not look down.
Be sincere and remember to learn from high and low
Just devote yourself to the way.

KENDO FOR ADULTS

By Hatano Toshio (Courtesy of Kendo Nihon)
Translated by Alex Bennett

Hatano Toshio-sensei was born in January 1945 in Musashi Murayama, Tokyo. After graduating from Kokushikan High School and Nihon University, he became a salaryman for a few years before establishing the Nanbudō Kendōgu shop in 1971. He passed the 8-dan exam on his second attempt in 1994. He serves as an advisor for the West Tokyo Kendo Federation, and is Suruga University Kendo Club Shihan, Musashi Murayama City Kendo Federation president, and leader of the Kinryūkan Dojo.

Part 1: Aspiring to do Correct Kendo

I run my own *bōgu* shop in Tokyo. As such, I am lucky if I can do *keiko* three times a week on average. I think that most people in the workforce can usually only manage once or twice a week due to work and family commitments. I currently serve as the president of the Musashi Murayama City Kendo Federation. Most of the members are company workers. Along with my own training, I am constantly thinking of how I can help them improve their kendo.

In this new series of articles, I will introduce various technical issues that can be addressed for mature kenshi. Before doing that, I would like to start by looking at the necessary frame of mind needed for improvement. This is probably the most important aspect for developing your kendo as you get older.

If you aspire to do "good kendo", promotion will come as a path of the course

I have always approached my training with the intention of doing "correct kendo". Many people concentrate on striking their opponent while avoiding getting struck themselves. This mindset leads to irritation when you do get hit by your opponent. If you can't get past that, you will end up getting the same advice you did a year ago. In other words, you will have the same problems and habits, and will not be able to advance.

One of the members in my federation competed in the High School National Tournament (Inter-High) in his younger days, but all he thinks about even now is scoring points on his opponents. I gave him the following advice: "If you persist in resorting back to your old tricks, your kendo will just keep going downhill. Just try and make your strikes straight. Maintain the same feeling that you had when competing in your high school days, but start doing kendo correctly."

At the following *keiko* session, he made an effort to strike straight, and I praised him in front of the others for trying to change his approach. "Well done for your brave attempt to do straight kendo. Even if you get hit over and over, your kendo will reach new heights after a year of practice as long as you are determined to do it properly. People will rate your kendo highly." The reality is, however, such a major overhaul is very hard to accomplish. Nobody wants to be hit, but if you are hell bent on not getting struck, fixing bad habits is no easy matter.

When I was still 7-dan, I was told that I would never pass the 8-dan examination doing what I was doing. I wasn't doing kendo for the sake of passing examinations anyway. I was just intent on doing "good kendo". It was this attitude that actually resulted in my passing the 8-dan examination. This applies to all ranks in kendo.

Become a regular team player in society, too

On the day I went to Kyoto to attempt the 8-dan examination, I awoke at 5:00am and paid my respects to my ancestors. I knew I had done everything I could to get to this stage, including looking after family matters and the like. I think that attention to detail in other aspects of your life helps to prepare your mind, and this is very important for getting your head in the right space for the examination. They say that kendo begins and ends with *rei* (respect), which is why I wanted to express my respect to my ancestors.

I have been involved with the former Seta kendo group in Gunma Prefecture for over 20 years. The region has since been absorbed by another town, but I still train with the old group a couple of times a year. There are about 40 members with 6- or 7-dan, and most are busily engaged in agriculture or farming chickens, pigs, and the like. They are all very keen on their kendo, to the extent that I am in awe of their drive.

One year, the president of the group brought two of his members who were preparing to sit the 6-dan examination to train with us in Musashi Murayama. When *keiko* started, one of them took it upon himself to stand as a *motodachi*, and the Musashi Murayama people formed a queue to fight him. They didn't know what rank he was, and even 6-dan holders were lining up to practise with him.

I was taken aback. Why on earth would a person who has come to a dojo as a visitor to learn be so arrogant as to stand in a position where others line up for him. I stopped him and said, "The person you are training with is a 6-dan. Have you no common sense at all?!" He passed the 6-dan examination not long after, and I was asked to attend the celebratory party. I was even asked to give a speech, which I did. "I respect the hard work you made to pass the test. But, allow me to make one comment. I find it very difficult to congratulate somebody who visits a dojo with the intention of learning, but then starts to teach instead. It is an embarrassment to the sensei who took you there as a guest. Why can you not understand this basic premise? And, why hasn't anybody pulled you up for this before? This kind of action runs counter to the meaning of doing kendo. You may have passed the AJKF's exam, but I don't recognise your 6-dan grade. Passing people with such a bad attitude is detrimental to kendo as a whole."

There was also an 8-dan sensei present, so I told him as well. "As an 8-dan sensei, you can't just be friends with your students. An 8-dan has got to say what needs to be said. Even if people hate you for it, if you don't speak your mind and rectify matters, then the whole kendo world suffers as a result."

Some days later, I received a letter from the new 6-dan. I replied that, although I had said some harsh things, I hoped he could accept my remonstrance with the grace with which it was given, and use it to keep growing as a person.

I also hold the position of Shihan for the kendo club at Surugadai University. I endeavour to teach students to be "regular team players for society" as well. "Regular players" are the select group who represent the university team at competitions. Not everybody can make it into the team. In the same spirit, though, I try to teach students that they need to have the "regular player" mindset in everything they do, especially when they graduate from university and try to make their way in the world. That means gaining the trust of others, and being seen as a necessary member of society. In the case of the university team, regardless of whether you are good enough to be a regular team member or not, everybody has to keep trying as hard as they can. If you are not selected, your job is to do all that you can to support the team. This is the kind of attitude that people appreciate, and rate highly in society at large.

I tell the students that once they enter the workforce, they should always arrive earliest at the company for their first year. People will know straight away that you are very enthusiastic about your work, and have a strong will to do well even if you are not good at it yet. Usually it is the company bigwigs who get to the office first, and they will be sure to notice. This is what I learned in my company days, and it is applicable to all things in life.

In any case, through the ensuing articles in this series, I will introduce various training methods and ideas to help mature kenshi develop their kendo. I will also include some poems that I composed over three decades ago to keep my mind focused. I will finish this introductory article with the first one.

わずかな差　気づかなければ　天地の差
(*Wazuka na sa, kizukanakereba, tenchi no sa*)
A tiny difference, Gone unnoticed, Is a world of difference.

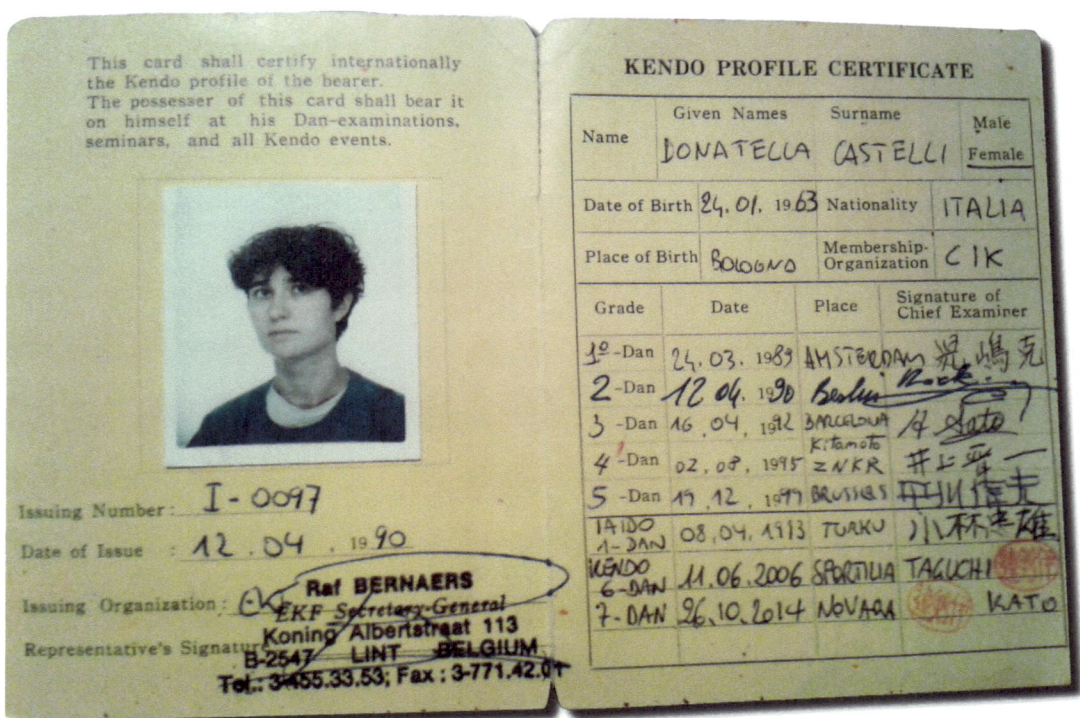

PASSING 7-DAN:
Reflections after the Facts

By Donatella Castelli

I passed 7-dan. I keep repeating it to myself, because I still fail to understand the consequences. I have been back to *keiko*, as usual, I and have been teaching and have been taught, so apparently nothing major has happened.

Nevertheless, it was a special event. I felt good during the examination, but I was sure I would not pass before stepping in front of the grading panel. I was inspired by the beauty of Furukawa-sensei's movements during practice the day before. The imagery helped, but I still have a long list of improvements I need to make, and I suppose I will never reach that ideal level even in a lifetime. Thus, passing 7-dan is, in truth, just an intermediate goal.

Of course, I have worked very hard for it, practically from the day after obtaining 6-dan. I know how quickly the years fly by, so I knew the next examination would be upon me in the blink of an eye. Training regularly, going to Japan every year to visit my *sensei*, having *keiko* in the dojo with friends and teachers who were also due to be take an examination – that has been my routine for the past eight years.

I passed all my examinations up to 5-dan on the first attempt. To get 6-dan, it took me six attempts over 18 months. During that time, my kendo changed significantly from the first to the sixth successful attempt. It was a revealing experience, and I relay it to everyone who is struggling with multiple failures. Failing is a powerful push to change, and you cannot get better if you do not change. Trying and failing can be the beginning of a journey of discovery, provided that change is actively pursued. Mere repetition for its own sake does not help improvement. It took me two years to pass 7-dan. I felt completely disoriented at the first attempt in Novara, but I had plenty of time to get ready for my recent successful grading in Novarello.

I spent the last year in Japan living, working and training, rehearsing the examination *tachiai* with other 7-dan candidates every week, under the eye of an 8-dan *sensei*. That was part of normal life in every dojo where I did *keiko* in Kyoto. I did the best I could but some days were better than others. I gathered all the possible pieces of advice I could from my *sensei* from Nara, Osaka, Gunma, Morioka, Tochigi, and Fukuoka. I wrote a lot of notes, but never read them. I already had enough on my mind to try and improve without consulting lists of faults to correct.

Of all the pieces of advice I received, two really had a profound effect:

An examination is like a play

Since time is very short you have to show the judges your best kendo, meaning your best posture, *waza*, and attitude from the very outset. Anything that does not contribute to showcasing your best is worthless, i.e. pushing, parrying, wasting time in *tsubazeriai*, or breaking your posture.

Strive to make your kendo a masterpiece, as a painter or a musician would do

Since you have dedicated so many of your resources, you have to give your best to honour the effort you put into it. Less than 100% will not do.

As you may notice, these pieces of advice are not concerned with technical details such as *tenouchi* or the angle of your knee in *kamae*. Such fine points should be taken care of in everyday practice, in every single *ji-geiko* or *kihon-waza* session, in the normal trial-and-error process that we all carry on in the dojo. These two suggestions relate more to the world of art, and possibly for this reason they particularly impressed me. Nothing could be further from sporting performance. Here we are talking about representing beauty through kendo. I think this can appeal to all of us and indicate a different meaning of a grading. Who knows, we may even grow to like it, instead of fearing it.

So, what next? As I mentioned, *keiko* goes on as usual. Although I am starting to think about the 8-dan examination, it is ten years away. I am looking forward to seeing the first (Japanese) lady pass this historic milestone first, and I have the honour of knowing some of the best candidates. On a more realistic note, I will go on practising as long as I can and keep encouraging ladies to do the same. If there was something that really pleased me in the messages I received from all over the world after my success, it was hearing that it has inspired other ladies and added to their resolve to follow the same path.

REI *DAN* *JI* *CHI*

THE GREATER MEANING OF KENDO

REIDAN-JICHI PART 18

WAZA BASICS

By Prof. Ōya Minoru (Kendo Kyōshi 7-dan)
International Budo University

Translated by Alex Bennett

Broadly speaking, there are two types of *waza*: "*shikakete iku waza*" and "*ōjite iku waza*." These categories are usually referred to as *shikake-waza* and *ōji-waza*, but I include the verb "*iku*" (go) in the middle to emphasise the importance of proactively making the opportunity to strike. *Shikakete iku waza* are techniques in which you instigate the motion, and *ōjite iku waza* are applied techniques to counter the opponent's strikes, adapting as they make an attack. They can be broken down into the following sub categories.

Before being able to execute an accurate and appropriate technique amidst the complex interaction between you and the opponent, the principles and laws of *shinai* manipulation must first be learned as the "basis for *waza*". After learning the principles and laws, controlling *maai*, identifying striking opportunities, and selecting the right *waza* to employ depending on changes in the opponent's movement are mastered through ongoing training. The scope in which various techniques can be applied successfully will broaden over time. In this article, and the following one, I will explain the mechanics of the most representative *waza*. I will start with the first two techniques in the *shikake waza*.

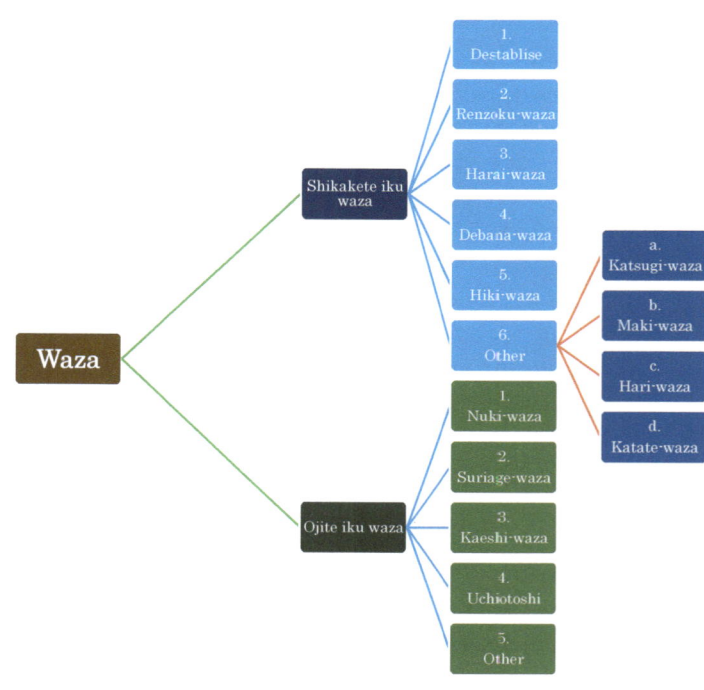

Shikakete iku Waza

1. Destabilising the opponent's *kamae* through *seme* and striking as they react

Here, I am referring to the act of destabilising the opponent's *kamae*, and striking when his *kensen* drops, rises, opens, or his hands move up. It is important to look at the opponent's eyes while also keeping his entire body in perspective, and striking the instant you detect an opening created through your *seme*.

Evoking a reaction and employing waza

Reaction here refers to an opening that manifests as the opponent's *kamae* is destabilised through applying pressure (*seme*). *Seme* can be summarised as taking the initiative with stronger *ki*, taking control of the opponent's centre, or moving into an advantageous *maai*. The strongest *seme* is achieved through proactively breaking through the opponent's centre and destabilising him. Thus, *ki*, the *kensen*, and the centreline all play an important part in the act of destabilising and creating an opening to strike. It should be noted that the *seme* being referred to here is not meant as a stratagem to "coax" your opponent.

It is vital to be ready at any time, physically and mentally, to strike immediately as you apply pressure. The grip of your left hand is instrumental in enabling this. Do not *seme* the opponent's centre only with your hands, and avoid having too much strength or tension in your upper body. The left hand must be solid and steady, and transmit your strength of will from your gut as you chip away at the distance between you and the opponent. The process of *seme*, causing a reaction/opening, and following through with a strike can be summarised as follows:

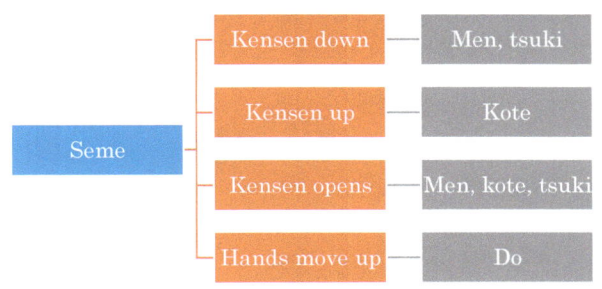

The instant your opponent reacts to your *seme*, vigorously follow through with a strike with a feeling of smashing his *shinai* with your chest. Use of the right foot is paramount in this process as it is the "*seme* foot", and it also seals the strike when it is made. The left foot is loaded and ready to thrust the body forward. The right foot slides across the floor as the opponent's centre is pressurised, and the distance is adjusted as an opportunity to strike is created. The opening is caught with the movement of the right foot as soon as it appears.

Even if the opponent attacks when you are engaged in *seme*, as long as the movement of your right foot is fluid, you can seamlessly manoeuvre to execute a counter technique. Or, if he retreats, adeptly close the gap by shuffling forward with the left foot. Depending on the opponent's reaction you can attack if they are overwhelmed, or continue to apply pressure.

Waza Options

Men-waza: When his *kensen* drops.
Kote-waza: When his *kensen* rises. *Kote* strikes should principally be executed over the opponent's *shinai*. However, if the *kensen* rises or opens too much, it is possible to strike from underneath.
Dō-waza: When his hands rise into the air.
Tsuki-waza: When his *kensen* drops or opens to the side.

Main Points

- *Seme* with the expectation that your opponent will react, and strike with total commitment (*sutemi*).
- Strike the appropriate target as the opponent reacts and an opening appears. It is not acceptable to strike *gyaku-dō* if the opponent's *kamae* has not been destabilised.

2. Renzoku-waza

There are two trains of thought regarding *renzoku-waza*. Strike the first target with all of your might, and if it is insufficient but the opponent is still reeling, then follow up immediately with a finishing blow. Or, make the

first strike with the intention of unsettling the opponent and setting up the next strike as they change positions. Regardless of the intention, each strike should be made with conviction and continued until a decisive blow is made. You must also be cognizant of the way the opponent is reacting to avoid striking randomly. Avoid striking in the same tempo, and use your feet well to adjust the *maai* as needed. It is relatively simple to make the transition from straight strikes (*men*, *kote*) to a side strike (*dō*); but the opposite is not so easy, and should be avoided.

Waza Options
(From *kote*)

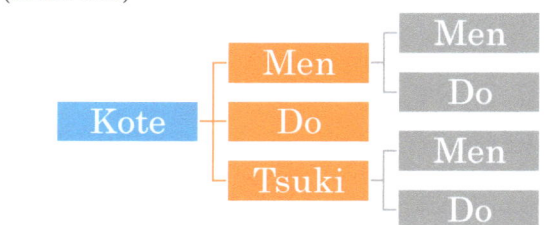

Kote-men: Look for the right moment to strike *kote*. When the opponent retreats lowering his hands, or opening his *kensen* to the side to try and avoid the *kote* attack, instantaneously strike *men*.

Kote-dō: Look for the right moment to strike *kote*. When the opponent tries to evade the strike by lifting his hands up, continue after *kote* with a strike to *dō*.

(From *men*)

Men-men: Look for the right opportunity to strike *men*. When the opponent retreats and drops his *kensen* down, or lurches back to avoid the *men* strike, follow through with another strike to *men*.

Men-dō: Look for the right opportunity to strike *men*. If the opponent raises their hands attempting to block the strike, follow through with another to *dō*.

(From *tsuki*)

Tsuki-men: Look for the right opportunity to thrust at the throat. If the thrust is inadequate, or it is deflected by the opponent, strike at *men* as they lean backwards to avoid the first attack.

Main Points
- Strike each target with total commitment (*sutemi*).
- Make the consecutive strikes swiftly. However, be sure not to strike too fast so that your posture becomes unbalanced and the strikes are inaccurate.
- To ensure immediate execution of the technique in accordance with the opponent's reaction, it is important that the left foot is snapped back into position after the first strike.

In my next article, I will outline the technicalities of the remaining *shikake waza*.

Japanese School Kendo and My Journey from Yokohama to the U.S.

By Ko Tabata *(Photos courtesy of Kendo Nihon and Denis Ralutin)*

Collecting the runner-up medal at the 2014 AUSKF Championships (Courtesy AUSKF – Dennis Ralutin)

I started kendo at the age of three in Kanagawa Prefecture, Japan, because my father used to run a junior high school kendo club. On January 31, 1994, while my father was doing kendo, he died of a heart attack aged only 37 years old. At that moment, even though I was only three, I decided to be a kendo champion someday. After my father's death, kendo became very special to me, and I still think of it as my inheritance from him.

My younger brother Yo and I were raised by our grandparents because my mother had to work long hours as a nurse in an elementary school. Our family was not well-off, living on only one salary, but my mother was always by my side and helped me in any way she could so I could realise my dream of becoming a kendo champion.

In 2002 and 2003, Toin Gakuen High School (TGHS) in Yokohama won the Inter-High (All Japan High School Championships). Once my mother and I heard that news, we realised that this would be the best school for my kendo. In April 2004, when I was 12 years old, I was accepted into Toin Gakuen Junior High School (TGJHS). I chose TGJHS because it would be easier to join the TGHS kendo team in the future. Even though Toin Gakuen was located in the same prefecture as my hometown, it was a little too far to commute to school every day before and after a hard practice. Therefore, at the age of 12, right after graduation from elementary school, I decided to live in the campus dorm. Obviously, living in the dorm with my friends was fun, but at the same time, it was one of the hardest periods of my life.

To give you an idea of what life in the dorm was like, here is a typical day:

06:30	Wake up for roll call. It was big trouble if I was not in the hall on time.
06:35–07:00	Cleaning time (bathroom, floors, stairs)
07:00–08:00	Morning training (two days a week)
08:00–08:20	Breakfast in the cafeteria
08:25–08:45	Morning homeroom
08:45	Classes start

There was not a moment to relax before going to school. I still remember running to class, sweating and eating bread and boiled eggs as I went so that I wouldn't be late. Usually, classes finished at around 15:10 every day. However, I do not remember anything of what I learned in class because I was asleep most of the time. I knew it wasn't right, but I could not help it because I was so tired from the morning tasks.

As a baby with dad   *At 13 years old*

In those days, TGJHS kendo club was not as strong as the TGHS club because it did not have a system to recruit good kendoka from all over the country like the high school did. Also, we only had practice after class four days a week from 16:00–18:00, which was a lot less than other strong junior high school kendo teams. However, I spent a lot of time watching the high school students practise when I didn't have training on Tuesday, Wednesday and Friday. Through watching my *senpai*, I became resolved to earn a starting position in the TGHS team and be a champion someday.

After lessons at TGJHS finished, this is what the rest of the day was typically like:

15:10	Classes finish
16:00 –18:00	Kendo practice. This consisted of stretching, *suburi*, *kihon-waza*, *ji-geiko* and *kakari-geiko*
18:30–19:00	Dinner in the cafeteria
19:00–19:30	Return to the dorm and take a bath
19:30	Roll call in the dorm lobby
19:30–21:00	Mandatory study in the study room
21:00–21:30	Small break (this was the only time I could talk to my mother on the pay phone)
21:30–23:00	Mandatory study time (the housemaster walked around the rooms to make sure that everyone was studying)
23:00	Lights out

Living in the dorm was very strict. We were not allowed to bring in TVs, games, *manga*, or any other kind of fun activity from home. All we could do was kendo and study. Even though we had a short break from 21:00–21:30, there was only one TV in the whole dorm, which had about 200 boys, including the high school baseball club students. Therefore, as a junior high school student, I could not watch the box.

This lifestyle was very hard for a 12- or 13-year-old boy, and I often wanted to go home, see my family, eat my grandmother's cooking, and just do things that normal junior high school students were doing. Having said that, I never regretted the choice to live there, and I believe that experience affected my life in a positive way. This was one of the biggest reasons why I could eventually move to the U.S. to study several years later on my own, without any anxiety.

After graduating from TGJHS, I moved into TGHS, which had one of the best high school kendo clubs in Japan. Tomita Takayuki-sensei, the high school kendo club manager, recruited so many strong kendoka from all over the country, from as far afield as Okinawa and Hokkaido, who were among the best in my generation. They started living in the dorm just like I did in junior high school. When I started TGHS, I originally thought that I would live in the dorm with my teammates in order to focus only on kendo, but as there was a huge difference in ability between them and myself at the beginning of high school, my mother and I felt that I could not become stronger than them if I did the same thing.

Therefore, my mother, brother and I moved into a small apartment close to school to let me focus on kendo. My mother could cook me meals every day, and I did not have to worry about anything other than kendo, unlike my teammates living in the dorm. I understood that this decision made things difficult for my family, which meant I had to be successful, whatever it took.

The TGHS team just before the final of the 2009 Inter-High
(Ko, far left / Courtesy Kendo Nihon)

Scoring a kote in the final of the 2009 Inter-High (Courtesy of Kendo Nihon)

The TGHS kendo team's practice was from 16:00–18:20, Monday to Friday, except Thursday, and on Saturday afternoons after morning classes. Thursday was a free practice day, and we did not have to do kendo, but everyone still trained on their own anyway. On Sundays we travelled to competitions or exhibition matches with other schools, so in reality, we trained seven days a week. Furthermore, the Japanese high school system does not have an off-season like in the U.S. That meant that we could not take any long periods off to go back home and spend time with our families. There were a couple of days off after the Inter-High at the beginning of August, and also from December 28 or 29 to January 1. Overall, we only had about 10 days off in the entire year. I think this is certainly very different from the kendo environment in other countries, but in order for us to be successful in competitions, it was necessary.

You might think the amount of practice is the biggest factor in Japanese kendo's continued strength and success. That is true to a degree, but it is not the only factor. The content of *keiko* is most likely different from that of other countries. Each school has its own original practice menu, but I will introduce that which we did at TGHS. I am so glad to have had Tomita-sensei as my coach. He created a unique practice that not only improved our technique, but also helped us to win.

Kendo is often thought of as being very strict in following traditional manners, but our practice at TGHS was totally different from that image.

16:00–16:15 Stretching.

This was done listening to loud hip-hop and pop music. In our dojo, there were big speakers mounted in the walls and ceilings. We even had a music committee to assemble new songs and put together a CD once a month.

16:15–16:30 *Suburi* with a heavy *bokutō*, also with music.

The type of *suburi* we did was;
Jōge-buri × 50
Shōmen-uchi × 50
Sayū-men-suburi × 50
Fumikomi-suburi (right and left *fumikomi*, one after the other) × 50
Kaikyaku-suburi (*suburi* with legs widely spread sideways) × 50
Haya-suburi × 100
Stretching and *suburi* were very important to get us ready physically and mentally, and the music helped us do that. Once *suburi* had finished, the music was turned off and we put our *men* on.

16:30–17:00 *Kihon-uchi*.

There were three people in one group, so one person could rest before actually making a strike.

In the semi-final against Simon Yoo at the 2014 AUSKF Championships (Courtesy of AUSKF – Dennis Ralutin)

Our *kihon-uchi* was basically the same as with any dojo, and it was not particularly challenging or hard. However, the priority in our team's practice was "quality". We tried so hard to make every single strike an *ippon* and not just go through the motions. If we missed a strike or were being lazy, our teammates pointed it out and yelled at us immediately. We had to do it with 120% *kiai* and motivation, which could be very tough, even for 30 minutes. However, it was very helpful.

17:00–17:10   Break

After *kihon-uchi* we took our men off and had a ten-minute break, but as everyone was in a serious mood, nobody talked or joked around.

17:10–17:45   *Shiai*-centric practice

Here we would practise one of the following things that would be very useful in shiai:

— Hiki-waza keiko: There were two courts, each with a referee and two players. The two players tried to get an ippon using only hiki-waza for one minute. This practice was very helpful to improve our hiki-waza and to see in what situations opponents tried to execute a waza from tsubazeriai.

— Tantō (short sword) defence practice: In a shiai, there were many situations in which we had to kill time in order to win or tie. However, this is very difficult to do. In order to overcome this weakness, we used a very short shinai, a little longer than a kodachi, about 20 inches. If you tried to defend with this sword, the opponent who was using a 3.8 length shinai could strike you. Therefore, you had to use good footwork to escape. This was a very good practice to learn what to do with a long shinai. With a short shinai, if you could keep your opponent from getting an ippon there should be no problem with a normal shinai. We did this in the same way as *hiki-waza keiko*, two courts for one minute.

— *Ippon-shōbu*: Again with two courts and one referee, this was a very good opportunity for everyone to show the coaches how good and strong we were.

— Last-minute-of-match *keiko*: This type of *keiko* had a very similar concept to the *tantō* defence practice. I am sure that sometimes you have had to get an *ippon* to win or tie in the last minute of a match. In order to win from that kind of situation, four B-Team boys were on one side, and four A-Team members on the other with one referee in each court. The A-Team members had to get an *ippon* within one minute. After one minute, the A-Team member moved to the next court and started again. The coach did not care what the A-Team members did. All they had to do was get an *ippon*. This practice was just like a real *shiai*. Sometimes, it was dangerous and hard because the A-Team members had to fight four consecutive times, but that was how we learned to win in a real competition.

17:45–18:15 *Ji-geiko*
This was done with the sensei and coaches. We then finished with *kirikaeshi* or *oikomi* from one end of the dojo to the other.

This was the typical practice menu in the TGHS kendo club. It may not be as crazy as many people might imagine. Some probably think Japanese high school students are always doing *kakari-geiko* and *oikomi* for hours on end. Of course, other good kendo teams still do that, but my kendo team was not like that at all. I can at least say that our practice was successful in keeping students concentrating on *keiko*, and to help them have a strong image of *shiai* all the time. I would say my high school practice was more like a Western sports practice than that of a traditional martial art. Recently, I feel that many schools have been starting this kind of training. It is very hard to define which one is better, but I think it is worth thinking about bringing this type of activity into your practice.

As mentioned above, I was a lot weaker than my teammates when I entered TGHS, so in order to get a starting position, I had to do extra training. I would run three miles a day in the morning, and then I practiced with my kohai until 07:30, so I had to wake up at 05:30 every morning. I would also run three miles after evening practice. That was what I had to do in order to become an A-Team member, something I was able to do when I became a senior. Doing extra training was very hard, but there was no choice if I wanted to reach my goal.

In August 2009, when I was a senior, TGHS placed second in the Inter-High in Osaka. Even though our team lost in the final, I was the only one of five members to win a match. I know that I didn't realise my dream 100 per cent, but I was confident that my family and my father in heaven would be satisfied with the result, just as I was.

High school was a big part of my life, but for the next stage I chose to study in the U.S. After accomplishing my kendo goal for the most part, I thought I needed to experience a new world, and to learn something different from kendo. From the age of three until coming to the U.S., most of my life had revolved around kendo. I had never studied hard, let alone had any interests other than kendo. To expand my horizons, I came to the U.S. to study at Southeast Missouri State University. I think it was a very good choice, as I have been able to meet many smart and talented students from all over the world. I think I have become wiser since coming to the U.S, but I have also found out how little I know about the world outside of kendo. Yet, I still have not been able to forget about kendo, even for a second.

I did not tell my mother, but since I came to the U.S. in 2010, I had been aiming to compete in the All United States Kendo Championships (AUSKC) in 2014. Unfortunately, my college was more than two hours away by car to the nearest place that I could do kendo, and I could only practise on average four times a year. However, I joined the judo club at my college and was able to train three times a week. Additionally, as I lived right next to a sports centre, I went to the gym and worked out for at least two and a half hours, four days a week for over four years. I was concentrating on making a habit of training constantly, just like in high school. This was all for the AUSKC in 2014.

In March 2014, during my journey to the 2014 AUSKC, I got third place in the National Collegiate Judo Championship -66kg division. I was very surprised by that result, but I think the reason I could do it, even though I only started judo since coming to the U.S., was because I knew how hard it is to win, how much effort I had to commit to win, and above all, how much I needed to win.

Three months later in San Diego at the 2014 AUSKC, I was runner-up in the men's individual competition. The result was not quite what I wanted, but I understood that winning was not that easy. There was another person who put in more commitment than I was able to. From June 28, 2013, to June 28, 2014, the day of AUSKC, I only did kendo six times, including one *shiai* and one try-out. Unfortunately, I could not get as many opportunities to train as I wanted, certainly not like in high school. Still, I believed that I was the one who practised and desired to be No. 1 the most. I pushed myself really hard, and never gave up on my goal. That second place came from commitment, I believe. My will was built through my kendo experience at Toin Gakuen.

The point that I would like to make is that, if you have that strong desire, you do not necessarily have to train with somebody—you can do it by yourself. The result does not depend on your environment or others, but yourself. I cannot give enough thanks to all the people who supported me in realising my dreams. From now on, my priority is to start passing on to others that which I have been taught.

"Jūbun no make wa Jūbun no kachi"

(Within a great deal of defeat there is a great deal of victory)

Higuchi Matashichirō Sadatsugu (?-?) *lived around the beginning of the Tokugawa period (1603-1868) and contributed greatly to the development of the Maniwa Nen-ryū*

"In the Maniwa Nen-ryū, trainees learn how to attain victory through trying to be beaten. This results in a natural win. Within a great deal of defeat there is great deal of victory."

Maniwa Nen-ryū is a traditional school of *kenjutsu* established in 1591 by Higuchi Matashichirō Sadatsugu (c. 16th century). It is almost solely practised in Maniwa Village, Yoshii Town, in modern day Gunma prefecture. The school stands out because of the fact it is mainly limited to one location, and it was traditionally studied by farmer-warriors (*gōshi*). And, the techniques are truly bizarre. Seventy percent of the training consists of *kata*, and around thirty per cent of full contact sparring. It was one of the first schools of swordsmanship to make use of *shinai*, or mock bamboo training swords, protective gloves, and an odd kind of headgear that is basically a cushion secured to the top of the head. They do not use *dō*.

The *kamae* is also characteristic with the hips lowered and most of the body weight placed on the back foot, with the front foot almost left floating in the air. The *kamae* were designed to give the opponent opportunities to attack. This falls in line with one of the important teachings of the school —"Within a great deal of defeat there is a great deal of victory."

Higuchi Sadatsugu became famous through a duel with Murakami Tenryū (Murakami Gosaemon) of the

By
ALEX BENNETT
Based on the book
"KENSHI NO MEIGON" (1998)
by the late Tobe Shinjūrō
Used with author's permission.

Tendō-ryū around 1600. The duel was sparked over who should be the alpha warrior in the region. There was not enough room for the Tendō-ryū and the Maniwa Nen-ryū to operate in the same locality. Tenryū sent letters challenging Sadatsugu to settle the matter with him once and for all. Sadatsugu refused to engage the Tendō-ryū hothead, but was coerced into action through constant taunts and insults about the feebleness of Nen-ryū followers.

A match was organized and the two faced off in a bamboo enclosure. Tenryū thought he had the upper hand and charged forth full of vigour and supreme confidence, only to headbutt Sadatsugu's wooden sword. Falling flat on his back, Sadatsugu put Tenryū out of his misery with a death blow to the head. Thus, Maniwa Nen-ryū prevailed from that time forth, and is still practised in the hills of Maniwa.

One of the remnants of this violent encounter is the legendary rock that Sadatsugu supposedly split in half after a few days and nights spent at the Yamana Hachiman shrine preparing for the battle. The stone is called "*tachiwari-ishi*" (rock rent asunder by a sword), and it is still located close to the current Maniwa dojo.

Although the Maniwa Nen-ryū does not seem nearly as sophisticated as other classical systems of swordsmanship, the curricula provides the student with a solid grounding in effective techniques for self-defence and counterattacking. Rather than take the role of aggressor, the underlying philosophy of the Nen-ryū teaches the benefit of "latter movement" known as "*go-no-sen*" in modern kendo. In this sense, it is a system that revolves around the idea of preserving life rather than seeking to take it.

One of the most famous skills once demonstrated in the Maniwa Nen-ryū is "*yadome-jutsu*". Practitioners stand in front of a bow wielding adversary and summarily cut down arrows fired their way from various distances. This practice was not designed as a practical battlefield protection measure, but more as a training method to encourage confidence and precision in timing.

The underpinning philosophy of being a defensive style is peculiar given the turbulent times. By letting enemies attack first they embraced the possibility of defeat, but turned this into a way for ultimate victory.

Historical Sightseeing

Text and photographs by Bruce Flanagan

Owari Province's icon of power and affluence - Nagoya Castle

Part 06 OWARI PROVINCE 尾張国

The three great leaders

Owari Province is a historical region of feudal Japan that once occupied the area that is now the western half of modern-day Aichi Prefecture, home of Nagoya City. Another historical region, Mikawa Province, originally formed what is now the eastern half of Aichi Prefecture. These two neighbouring provinces were the birthplaces and proving grounds for the three great warlords of the Warring States Period: Oda Nobunaga, Toyotomi Hideyoshi and Tokugawa Ieyasu, the three historical figures now known collectively as the *san-eiketsu*, the 'three great leaders'. Owari Province commanded a central location in Japan's main island of Honshu and possessed stations on both the Nakasendō and the Tōkaidō travel routes, two of the five most significant travel paths of the Edo Period. The area also served as a hub of financial and political activity and boasts a long and turbulent history. Significant battles waged in the province include the Battle of Okehazama and the Battle of Komaki and Nagakute. Numerous landmarks and ruins remain today attesting to the area's eventful history. Modern-day Aichi Prefecture remains an affluent area of commerce and trade with Nagoya Port at its bustling centre. Aichi Prefecture is home to the Toyota Motor Corporation, porcelain tableware company Noritake and power tool company Makita. Chubu International Airport was constructed to the south of Nagoya when the prefecture played host to World Expo 2005.

Oda Nobunaga
織田信長
(1534-1582)

Toyotomi Hideyoshi
豊臣秀吉
(1537-1598)

Tokugawa Ieyasu
徳川家康
(1542-1616)

Daimyō of the Oda family ruled Owari Province during the Warring States Period. A castle called Nagoya Castle (那古野城),[1] which predates the later Nagoya Castle (名古屋城), was built in the province and was guarded by military general Oda Nobuhide. It was here in this castle that Nobuhide's son, Nobunaga, was born into power and affluence in 1534.

At the age of 26, Nobunaga defeated Imagawa Yoshimoto in the Battle of Okehazama in 1560 (the historical area known as Okehazama sat on the border between what is now modern-day Nagoya City and Toyoake City). Nobunaga amassed more power and land and based himself in Kiyosu, an area north-west of Nagoya, where he occupied Kiyosu Castle for a time before moving his seat of power to Gifu Castle. In 1568 he placed Ashikaga Yoshiaki as the *shōgun* in Kyōto but later destroyed Yoshiaki's military government by force in 1573.

He built Azuchi Castle on the shore of Lake Biwa and laid preparations for unifying the provinces (*tenka-tōitsu*) but took his own life when he was attacked by Akechi Mitsuhide's troops at Honnō-ji Temple in Kyoto in 1582.

Toyotomi Hideyoshi was born in the Nakamura area of Nagoya in 1537 to foot soldier Kinoshita Yaemon.[2] In his teens, after many changes of name, Hideyoshi served Matsushita Yukitsuna.

Before the age of 30 he became a servant to Oda Nobunaga but he was soon promoted to positions of higher import. His influence grew, and, under the name of Hashiba, he did battle with Akechi Mitsuhide, killing him in the Battle of Yamazaki. He brought the regions of Shikoku, Hokkoku, Kyūshū, Kantō and Oū under unified peace and built Osaka Castle. He fought Oda Nobukatsu and Tokugawa Ieyasu in the Battle of Komaki and Nagakute in 1584 and was defeated, but, with his enormous political power, he negotiated for Ieyasu to become one of his vassals.

In 1585 he became *Kanpaku* (Imperial Regent) and in 1586 received the name 'Toyotomi' from the Imperial Court. Later becoming *Daijō-daijin* (Chancellor of the Realm), he passed the title of *Kanpaku* to his adopted son (and nephew by blood) Hidetsugu and assumed the influential role of *Taikō* (Retired Regent). Hideyoshi launched two invasions to Korea before dying of illness in 1598.

Tokugawa Ieyasu was born to castle keeper Matsudaira Hirotada in Okazaki Castle, Mikawa Province in 1542 (Okazaki lies to the south-east of Nagoya). After a number of first-name changes, Ieyasu took the surname Tokugawa in 1566.

He served Imagawa Yoshimoto, later joined forces with Oda Nobunaga, and became a vassal of Toyotomi Hideyoshi after the Battle of Komaki and Nagakute in 1584. In 1590 he was given control of the eight provinces making up the Kantō region and occupied Edo Castle.

In 1600 he defeated the forces of Ishida Mitsunari and Mōri Terumoto in the Battle of Sekigahara and in 1603 created the Edo *bakufu* making him the first Tokugawa shogun. He was succeeded as shogun by his son Tokugawa Hidetada in 1605 but retained military power. In 1607 he decimated the Toyotomi clan in the Siege of Osaka, which laid the foundations for approximately 260 years of Tokugawa rule. Ieyasu died of illness in 1616.

Tōkaidō Road

(▶mlit.go.jp/road/michi-re/3-1.htm)

The Tōkaidō (Eastern Sea Road) was one of the five main travel routes in Honshū at the time of the Edo *bakufu*. The road began in Nihonbashi in Edo and ended in Kyōto making it the most important road of the five. It passed through many *daimyō*-controlled provinces and had 53 rest stations. Owari Province held two stations on the road; Narumi and Miya. The station at Miya was named so for being close to Atsuta Shrine. The next most important road of the time was the Nakasendō (Central Mountain Road) with 69 stations which also began and finished in the same place as the Tōkaidō but passed through rural Honshū rather than running along the coast. The Tōkaidō and the Nakasendō were connected by a smaller road of nine stations called the Minoji which began at Miya station. The Minoji passed through Nagoya and Kiyosu and various important rural locations and connected with the Nakasendō at Tarui-station in what is now Gifu Prefecture.

Nagoya Castle

(▶nagoyajo.city.nagoya.jp)

Located on the Minoji road, Nagoya Castle was built in 1610 by Tokugawa Ieyasu for his son Yoshinao to head the prestigious Tokugawa Owari-line, one of the three Tokugawa family branches. Construction of the castle was aided by Owari-born military commander Katō Kiyomasa. Although differing ranking criteria exist, Nagoya Castle is generally considered to be one of three most

Kiyosu Castle

Golden killer whale (kin-shachi)

significant castles in Japan. Two golden statues of killer whales (*kin-shachi*) adorn the castle's main tower. The castle was restored after severe damage by fire in World War II and the *kin-shachi* has now become a popular symbol of Nagoya City.

Kiyosu Castle

(▶kiyosujyo.com)

Kiyosu Castle was built by Shiba Yoshishige in 1405 approximately 5km north-east of and predating the original Nagoya Castle. Oda Nobunaga moved from the original Nagoya Castle to occupy Kiyosu Castle in 1554 for 8 years before moving to Komaki-yama Castle. In 1560 he lead his forces from their base at Kiyosu Castle to victory in the Battle of Okehazama against Imagawa Yoshimoto and laid the foundations for the unification of the provinces (*tenka-tōitsu*).

Inuyama Castle

(▶inuyama-castle.jp)

Inuyama Castle was built in 1537 by Oda Nobuyasu, an uncle of Oda Nobunaga. Naruse Masanari took over as castle guardian in 1617. Even though the picturesque castle did not play a significant role in Owari Province history, it remains undamaged in its original form and has received national treasure (*kokuhō*) status.

The Battle of Okehazama

(▶okehazama.net)

In 1560 Oda Nobunaga led 3000 troops against the 25,000 troops of Imagawa Yoshimoto in what is known as perhaps the most successful surprise attack in Japanese history. Imagawa and his troops had arrived and were camping in Okehazama where many were drinking in celebration of their expected victory due to superior manpower. Instead of a frontal attack using the main Tōkaidō road, Oda snuck up on Imagawa's encampment using mountain paths under the cover of heavy rain. Oda's troops burst into the camp scattering the drunken soldiers, stormed Imagawa's tent and decapitated him. Two ancient battlefield sites (*konsenjō*) remain today, one in Nagoya City's Midori-ku and another close by in Toyoake City. The former has been turned into a memorial park.

The Battle of Komaki and Nagakute

(▶md.ccnw.ne.jp/seinen/rekisikan/gaiyou.htm ▶nagakute-kankou.com/rekishi/komakinagakute.html)

In 1584 Toyotomi Hideyoshi (at the time Hashiba Hideyoshi) battled with the combined forces of Oda Nobukatsu and Tokugawa Ieyasu in the two Owari Province sites of Komaki and Nagakute. Hideyoshi's forces were defeated but, through diplomatic negotiations, Hideyoshi was able to gain the allegiance of Tokugawa Ieyasu who took on vassal (*shinzoku*) status to Hideyoshi's authority. This move increased Ieyasu's fame

Inuyama Castle

The hongū main shrine of Atsuta Shrine

Owari Kan-ryū practitioners perform ji-geiko with kuda-yari and modified kendo bōgu

and furthered Hideyoshi's plans for unification of the provinces. Komaki-yama Castle was built in 1563 and served as the battle position for Ieyasu's troops in the conflicts. A re-creation of the castle has now been constructed at Mount Komaki in modern-day Komaki City. The site of the Nagakute battle has now been turned into a park and history museum. Nagakute Town hosted the World Expo in 2005.

Atsuta Shrine
(▶atsutajingu.or.jp/jingu)

Atsuta Shrine is located in Atsuta-ku in Nagoya City. The history of the shrine is said to date back some 1900 years. Historically a station called Miya existed on the Tōkaidō road for visitors to access the shrine. It has provided a place of worship for a number of significant deities enshrined there and is said to house the Grass-cutting Sword (*Kusanagi-no-Tsurugi*), one of the three Imperial Regalia (*Sanshu-no-Jingi*). Atsuta Shrine is immensely popular and sees over 8 million visitors annually.

Owari Kan-ryū Sōjutsu
(▶nihonkobudokyoukai.org/marti-alarts/050)

Owari Kan-ryū is a martial arts school native to Owari Province. It is a *koryū* weapons system recognized by the Nihon Kobudō Kyōkai and is famous for its unique style of spearmanship (*sōjutsu*). The founder of the style was Tsuda Gonnojō Nobuyuki who is said to have founded Kan-ryū in 1671. The school employs 3.6m long spears called *kuda-yari*. In their front hand the spearman holds a short cylindrical metal tube called a *kuda*. The shaft of the spear feeds through this tube with each thrust and prevents wooden splinters from sword cuts piercing the spearman's hand. Practitioners don *bōgu* and practise *ji-geiko* against each other with *kuda-yari*. The 13th headmaster of the school is Katō Isao who runs the school's privately-owned *honbu-dōjō* located in Nakagawa-ku, Nagoya City.

Yagyū Shinkage-ryū Heihō
(▶yagyu-shinkage-ryu.jp)

The esteemed *koryū* style Yagyū Shinkage-ryū Heihō is based in Nagoya where training is supervised by the 22nd headmaster, Yagyū Kōichi. The style's fame stems from the fact that Yagyū swordsmen provided *kenjutsu* instruction to the Tokugawa family. Historically the Yagyū clan was divided into two branches, the Owari branch and the Edo branch, but the Owari branch maintains the school's original lineage. Practitioners train in classical *kenjutsu* using *fukuro-shinai* (a.k.a. *hikihada-shinai*) and in the *iai* techniques of Seigō-ryū battō-jutsu.

Bō-no-te
(▶lets-go-aichi.jp/article/2010/000576.html)

There are a number of weapon systems known as *bō-no-te* that have their historical roots in Owari and Mikawa Provinces. It is believed that the *ryūha* started when farmers and commoners were taught self-defence skills employing weapons such as staves, spears, *naginata*, swords, and sickles by the military instructors of their lords. Many of the teachings were documented in scrolls and continue to be handed down as regional heritage but over time the techniques were turned into prearranged dance performances dedicated to bringing good harvests. People of all ages from these communities can now practise the art's techniques and perform in festivals at local shrines. A considerable number of *ryūha* still exist that have been maintained by preservation groups and have now been classified as intangible folk culture assets of Aichi Prefecture.

Further reading and related sightseeing

Meiji-mura and the Museidō Dojo (see Kendo World 4.2), the Tokugawa Art Museum, Nagoya Festival, and Nagoya's Toyokuni Shrine.

Notes

1. Historically Nagoya (名古屋) was written with the characters 那古野, and occasionally 名護屋.
2. Some historians believe the year was 1536.

Bibliography

1. *Heisei Dai-gappei Nihon Shin-Chizu*, Masai Y., Shōgakukan Inc., 2005.
2. *Kōjien Dai-go-Han*, Iwanami Shoten, 2004.
3. *Aichi-ken no Rekishi (Kenshi #23)*, Miki S. (ed.), Yamakawa Shuppansha Ltd., 2001.
4. *Aichi-ken no Rekishi Sanpo (Jō - Owari) Rekishi Sanpo #23*, Aichi-ken Kōtō-Gakkō Kyōdo-shi Kenkyūkai (.ed), Yamakawa Shuppansha Ltd., 2005.
5. *Rekishi Gunzō - Meijō Shiriizu #4 - Nagoya-Jō*, Tamaru N., Gakushū Kenkyūsha, 1995.

Empty Mind Films:

An Interview with Martial Arts Documentary Filmmaker Jon Braeley

By Michael Ishimatsu-Prime

Empty Mind Films' Jon Braeley

Briton Jon Braeley is possibly the pre-eminent martial arts documentary filmmaker working in the world today. His catalogue includes *The Shaolin Kid: A Boy in China*, *Art of the Japanese Sword*, *Masters of Heaven and Earth*, and *The Zen Mind* to name but a few. Now based in Miami, Florida where he runs Empty Mind Films, his production company, he has made many documentaries on Japanese and Chinese martial arts, as well as Eastern spirituality and medicine. Braeley's latest work sees him venture for the first time into a series format that covers the Japanese budo arts. Kendo World caught up with him during the editing stage of the series that will feature kendo.

Kendo World: *The first episode of your new series, Warriors of Budo, went on sale in October 2014. Can you give us an overview of the series, what is it about, what can we expect to see?*

Jon Braeley: Initially, the idea was to make an updated version of the BBC documentary series from the 1980s called *The Way of the Warrior*, which covers the main arts that are designated as budo by the Nippon Budokan, such as aikido, karate, Shorinji Kempo, and kendo. We also wanted to introduce one or two new masters that represent different aspects of those arts.

In the new series we decided to start with karate because it will show the history of the martial arts a little bit easier than, for example, kendo, whose history remains firmly rooted in Japan. However, karate came from China, and in fact, India before that. We therefore thought that we would feature karate as the first episode, specifically Okinawan karate, with Higaonna Morio-sensei, 10-dan karate master of Gōjū-ryū who was actually in the original The Way of the Warrior BBC series. In the first 20 minutes of the program we show the history of the martial arts from the Shaolin Temple to *tai ji quan* (*tai chi*), and then how they came into Okinawa, and from there into mainland Japan. Even today, budo arts like karate, judo and Shorinji Kempo are still influenced by the Chinese martial arts on which they are based, and aikido to a certain extent, too.

The second episode will be on mainland karate. We had to dedicate two episodes to karate because of the number of styles, and also because it's the most popular martial art in the world. We have got one of the Japan Karate Association's former top instructors, Yahara-sensei, who split away to form a new association called "Karate-no-Michi". From the JKA we have Naka-sensei, who starred in a movie called *Kuro Obi* (Black Belt) and *High Kick Girl*. Naka-sensei allowed us to feature behind the scenes interviews on movie sets and showed us how martial arts are filmed in the movies. Wadō-ryū karate will be also featured at their Hombu Dojo where the current head, Ōtsuka Hironori gives a terrific demonstration of how to defend against a live blade or *shinken*.

Episode three will be aikido, specifically Yoshinkan aikido; episode four will feature Shorinji Kempo; episode five, judo and jujitsu; and episode six will be on kendo, and it will also feature naginata, jukendo, tankendo and

Higaonna Morio-sensei for WoB — *Ōtsuka Hironori-sensei for WoB* — *With Kanazawa Hirokazu* — *Wu style tai chi, HK, 1977*

iaido. Jodo is not featured yet but we're trying to arrange that now. It's currently six episodes, but it could end up becoming seven. Most of the footage has been shot, but we still have a little bit of kendo left to shoot. If I'm being optimistic, all the episodes should be screened within 12 months.

Each individual episode will be feature-length; the time will just run itself. Aikido is about 75 minutes and I think that the kendo episode will end up about that as well. The reason why it's an episode series, unlike the feature length format that I usually make, is because when they are finished, they will be edited into 60-minute episodes for TV. Many satellite and cable companies in Europe and Australia have already shown an interest in this series.

KW: *I saw in the preview that for the kendo episode you filmed in K8-dan Ozawa Hiroshi-sensei's dojo, Kōbukan.*

JB: That's right. We did a very big interview with him that lasted for about 2.5 hours. I love his dojo, it's beautiful. We filmed some *koryū* there as well as a kendo lesson.

KW: *What does Ozawa-sensei discuss in his interview?*

JB: He actually discussed 21-year-old Takenouchi Yūya's victory in the recent All Japan Kendo Championships. While he was watching his matches, he was wondering how he would be able to face someone like that who is younger, faster and physically stronger than him. He said that he would have to keep his *kamae* and maybe do a *kaeshi-dō*. That would be preferable to *debana-waza* because of the speed of Takenouchi's reactions.

KW: *Does the kendo episode focus on a specific aspect of the art? What did you want to show about kendo?*

JB: Rather than focus on one aspect of kendo, we instead show it in relation to the other sword arts and weapons with *koryū*, as well as jukendo and tankendo, jodo and naginata. There is also iaido. For the kendo itself we filmed across two All Japan Kendo Championships and two class practices, along with a number of annual *taikai* and *enbu*, so there is a lot of varied kendo content.

KW: *Did you film any kendo elsewhere?*

JB: We have also filmed *keiko* at Haga-ha Dojo at the Nippon Budokan. They do old, pre-war style kendo, and when they get going they end up doing jujutsu and start throwing each other. They have never opened their practice to film crews, but through a lot of contact with them, including sending them samples of our previous releases to show that we make serious documentaries, we were given permission to film them in November. They have seen our approach and know that we want to see the traditional side of the martial arts. We don't want to exaggerate or sensationalise the martial arts. We just want to show what they are.

We interviewed Uki Terukuni-sensei of Haga-ha. He said that a live blade is called a *"shinken"*. That word is also used in modern Japanese to describe being serious about something. Therefore, everyone is his dojo, even beginners, uses a *shinken*.

He doesn't feel that there are such things as *kobudō* (old-style budo) or *kobujutsu* (old-style martial arts). If the *iai* and kendo from the actual period are practised without forgetting its origin and essential spirit, there is no need for such words as "old".

KW: How many countries and locations are featured in Warriors of Budo?

Haga-ha Dojo kendo practice for WoB

JB: Japan, China and India. India was only featured in the karate episode as there is an Indian martial art called *kalaripayattu*, which is an early version of Shaolin *gong fu* (kung fu). When you look at this early martial art you can actually see pieces of kata that they still do in Okinawa today that are identical.

KW: *In the past you have covered different arts from different countries like Japan and China. Even though there are these differences, do you approach the subject in the same way?*

JB: Kind of, yes. There's a big overlap, and I think that when you train in a Japanese martial art like kendo or aikido, and to a certain extent karate, you get a little bit blinkered because they're very specific martial arts. I used to be like that until I started to make films. When you go to China and see the hundreds and hundreds of martial arts styles there, there's a huge overlap between them and you see very similar techniques and teaching methods as you see in Japan. I was surprised many years ago to see that and I'm still uncovering it now. I still go to the Shaolin Temple and see a monk teaching something that looks like aikido. I believe that if you were to give a *shinai* to a Shaolin monk, he would know what to do if facing a kendoka. They are very similar, and they teach things like jodo, so we do approach things in a similar way. I think that in Japan the martial arts are much more ordered, and that comes from centuries of a very orderly way of doing things. There used to be many more schools of *kenjutsu* than there are today that had very specific techniques and training methods, whereas in China, it's much more chaotic. What you would call a *ryūha* in Japan is probably what you would call a family in China with the same name. For example, the Chen family would all do Chen Tai-chi in a village called Chen. Or *ba gua zhang* which includes a sword form using a very broad sword, but it is specific to a family group. It's very muddled like that in China, and there are hundreds of different lineages. But in Japan it's very orderly and specific.

KW: *You don't have experience in all the martial arts that you cover, so is that a hindrance when making a documentary?*

JB: It can be a hindrance, but also a plus. My naivety about a certain art can make me ask questions that might be overlooked by someone who practises that art. We aim our documentaries at people who have an interest in martial arts and who maybe have never seen a martial arts program before. Therefore, we want to come into the dojo and say, "Tell us what you are doing." However, if you have an experienced background in kendo, for example, you might miss things that would be important to people with no experience.

I obviously get advised on what questions we should ask; I don't want to appear to be an idiot. We also have

Ozawa Hiroshi-sensei at Kōbukan for WoB

to be careful when editing. Although I have a karate background and have practised it for almost all my life, when we were in Okinawa filming Gōjū-ryū karate, even though I practised that style for a while, I still sought the advice of some Gōjū-ryū practitioners during the editing stage. My assistants are chosen carefully for the skills they bring to the shoots, for example Juandiego Fonseca in Japan who practises both kendo and kyudo and is invaluable as a member of our film crew.

I don't think it's impossible if you have no experience to make a documentary. I think that it's more important to have the philosophical and conceptual background of the art when you enter a dojo. You need to know the etiquette of the dojo when you go there, something that is more important in Japan than China. It is also important knowing the way to deal with a master of the art. For example now, with the Shaolin Temple in China, you cannot just go there and film anymore. They have stopped everyone. I was able to film there in February because I have an insider – a new assistant who was born in the temple and whose mother works there as a guide. I didn't use my usual assistant who has worked for me eight years full-time. I think that is more important than knowing the specific martial arts.

You also need to be able to approach the subjects in a manner that shows respect, not asking stupid questions like, "Have you got the death touch?" I actually just received a very nice email from the head of Higaonna-sensei's Australian dojo. He saw the documentary we just released on karate and he said that it is the best documentary he has seen that has featured Higaonna-sensei because we put the viewer into the dojo without any distractions. We just let the lesson flow, and if Higaonna-sensei wanted to say something into the camera we let it happen. We are trying hard to put the viewer in the dojo to experience the class as it unfolds. That was our philosophy with Warriors of Budo.

KW: *What is difficult or challenging about filming martial arts?*

JB: Right now the challenge is physical. In three days I'm heading to Wudang Mountain, China, and I'm nervous because it's really backbreaking. My two camera bags weigh about 50kg and going up and down that mountain is going to be quite stressful. Bending down over a camera for about six or seven hours is hard.

With regards to the actual filming, we have often been complimented about how we do not get in the way when we film, and people have said that they hardly know that we are there. Higaonna-sensei in Okinawa said that when he looked at us, I always seemed to have the camera pointing in the right direction. That's important – having the camera pointing in the right place. If it's not, the instructor or the teacher will realise that you don't know what you're doing.

The actual shooting itself is not so different from how you would shoot anything else. Focusing is difficult because I do it manually. I am from the old-school where you shoot with your hand constantly on the focus ring. We shoot hours and hours of material, and out of five or six hours of footage, if we're lucky, we might get ten or fifteen minutes out of it. Getting good audio is also very challenging, and also the look of the dojo. Japanese dojo are damp and the lighting is often fluorescent which does not yield a nice image. It can cause a flicker on the camera so you have to change the frame-rate to avoid cycle phasing. In China, they all train outside and it is nice to have natural lighting.

KW: *Is there a standout sensei or teacher that you have interviewed?*

JB: There have been so many, and I don't want to list too many karate *sensei*, but one is Kanazawa-sensei, one of the original instructors who left Japan to teach overseas. I did a very interesting interview with him in 2003; he was a very humble man. I think that with most of the top *sensei*, their humility is amazing. They deny their prowess in the arts, and say it's just training and that anybody can do what they do – you just have to put the hours in. We all know that's not true, there's only so much technique that you can learn. After a certain point it comes down to the strength of your mind. It is will and determination and your approach, and some of the top teachers exhibit that.

When it comes to the top masters, we are very lucky that we have been able to interview those at the very top of each art. It was one of the principles that we started Empty Mind with – if we can't get number one, we might settle for number two, but not three. The very first martial arts interview that we did was with aikido's Ueshiba Moriteru-sensei, the grandson of the founder, Ueshiba Morihei.

This is what I think sets us apart from our competition. If you look at some of the American TV programs, many of them do not seek out the top masters for a particular reason. It is because quite often when you interview people at the top, they tend to not really need to say too much, and in fact, the interviews can sometimes be a little boring. They don't need to sensationalise or capitalise on who or what they are, and use their position and strength to inflate their ego. So in fact, sometimes those types of interviews do not yield what a TV audience will want to see. Therefore, National Geographic and Discovery Channel tend to interview people lower down, who kind of have words fed into them and are somewhat manipulated, something

With Kayla Harrison, U.S. Olympic judo gold medalist, for WoB

which I have accused filmmakers of doing many times.

In *Warriors of Budo*, we went to Massachusetts to interview Kayla Harrison, the U.S.'s first gold medal judoka. She won gold at the 2012 London Olympics. She was incredible. We are always trying to find women in our martial arts documentaries; we don't want them to be full of testosterone.

KW: *Are there any arts that you have not yet covered that you would like to?*

JB: I have wanted to film Muay Thai boxing for a number of years. We got approved by the World Boxing Council in Bangkok in 2006. We were due to film but that was when a big tsunami hit which wiped out the training camp where we were supposed to go. All the kickboxers fight in Bangkok in the arenas, but they actually train and live in the islands in the South where it is cheaper. We scheduled it again and then it got cancelled by the government due to political problems.

There are still some small martial arts in China that I'd like to cover, but there are literally hundreds and I can't cover them all. We're going back to Wudang Mountain where I made a documentary called *Masters of Heaven and Earth*. We're going to cover it from a different angle and cover the health aspect of *qi gong* and its internal breathing and relate that to medicine, but there will also be some martial arts in it, too. It will be called *The Immortal Path*.

With regards to Japan, I don't think that we have covered kendo enough, and some of the other sword arts, but we're trying to do that now.

I'd also like to do sumo but that is proving to be difficult what with the politics involved. Sumo is split

At the All Japan Kendo Championships, 2014

into two: professional and amateur. On the professional side, film crews were banned because of all the scandals, corruption and bribery. They always think that you're going in there with an agenda, or to try and expose something. We approached the sumo federation and said that we're only interested in sumo as a martial art. They said that it wasn't a very good time — apparently there was some "house cleaning" going on. We also experienced the same thing at the Kodokan when we were trying to film judo there. At first we got flatly refused, due to some internal issues. Some people got fired and the government had threatened to come in and sort the organisation out. We were asked to wait six months, which we did, and in the end managed to get permission. We'd probably be able to film amateur sumo, but really, we want to film the professional side of it. As I've said before, I don't want to settle for second best, and as sumo is also a professional sport, I want to film that.

KW: *What made you give up a stable job as an architect to become a documentary maker?*

JB: I was an architect in the north of England for about 12 years. I gave that stability up, and England, too. I felt it was about time for a change, a *cliché*, I know. I left England for a new challenge and moved to New York. I worked as an architect there for a little while. I had always been a photographer – a passion I had in England not related to work. I was always taking photographs, and had studied it at university when I did a Fine Arts and Photography course, before I switched to architecture. Another passion I had was karate, which I started when I was 15 years old and have basically never stopped. I did other martial arts in England, too. I did aikido for a year and *tai chi* for a couple of years when I was 20, and even went to Hong Kong to study there.

I never thought that my passions for photography and martial arts would join together, but that's what happened. I moved to New York in 1990 and worked there for five years and then moved down to Miami. In 1997 I made my first documentary, but it was not related to the martial arts. It was about a Russian Olympic coach who was teaching Russian Olympic athletes but then defected. He came to the U.S. and taught a new method of running.

In 2000, an interesting thing happened. I got a call from a TV production company and they asked me to introduce them to martial arts people that I knew because I travelled around a lot to train. It turned out that I didn't do it because I checked them out and they were part of a well-known cable television channel. Everybody said that I should do be doing that myself; that provided the spark that created Empty Mind Films back in 2001. Instead of doing it as a hobby, I decided to do it properly. I had a photography studio at that time in Miami and I got rid of everything and switched to video, went on a training course in Los Angeles at Paramount Studios where they did a one-week boot camp to train filmmakers. I went on a few of those and then felt empowered enough to come to Japan to start making documentaries, that was the beginning of the first documentary—*The Empty Mind*—that was released in 2003. It was a bit ambitious because we wanted to connect all the top masters in one documentary. I felt that if you were to take a top martial arts teacher from Japan and one from China, and put them side by side, they could finish each other's sentences. They are so similar in their attitude, their knowledge, the way they teach, everything. We felt that a lot of people don't see that link between the top instructors. We travelled across Japan and filmed karate, aikido and other arts, and then we went to China to the Shaolin Temple in 2003. Also, I went to Wudang Mountain, a very famous martial arts location, which is where I'm going again in a few days.

KW: *Can you please elaborate more on your martial arts background?*

JB: I started karate when I was 15 years old. I came from a very tough neighbourhood in the north of England. We were very poor and I had five brothers who all went to work in the steel factories. You had to be able to look after yourself – that or be a very fast runner. I started karate because I was scared of getting beaten up. My confidence was so low at that point, so I liked having the skills to be able to deal with people if I got into a situation.

One of my brothers was in a band, and it just so happened that his manager was a black belt in karate. Once a week he would take me to the local YMCA to teach me karate. For the first year it was just the two of us. I was too shy to join a club, and I didn't have the means to do so anyway. A year later he then found me a club and that was when I really realised, "Oh wow, this is amazing." I was 16 at that time and had a part-time job, working my way through school. My first teacher was Roy Stanhope, and he is still the international coach in England. He was a legend in my hometown, driving a Lotus.

Bruce Lee and the program *Kung Fu* with David Carradine were all the rage at that time, so all the exposure to martial arts at that time came from China, like kung fu, never Japanese arts. However, in England, the only martial arts teachers then were Japanese. There was very little kung fu to be learnt in England. I naturally went to karate as that was the most popular one, that and judo. I did Shotokan karate, which is probably the most popular form of karate in the world, and it really paved the way for the martial arts to spread internationally.

KW: *Your background is karate, but have you got an interest in starting one of the other arts that you have covered?*

JB: I have a great feeling for aikido. As you get older, your art becomes more relaxed and softer. When I was young, my karate was all about strength, that was the Shotokan karate way—one punch to win. As you get older you realise the potential that being soft has and it can be advantageous. Your speed can increase with softness and your movements get better. For that reason, I have an interest in aikido.

I would love to do kendo, but the main reason that I'm not is because I couldn't carry the equipment around! I always felt that the true essence of the martial arts is that you should be able to do them in your clothes. Therefore, I have always been drawn to the weaponless martial arts like karate, aikido and judo.

KW: *What other projects are you working on at the moment?*

JB: We always have two or three projects running at the same time. Beside *Warriors of Budo* and *The Immortal Path* which I have mentioned, I shot a movie in India in 2013 about UFC champion Jonathan Brookins who was very jaded with the MMA scene, even though he won the final of the UFC a year before. He was burnt out with the fight scene, as well as fighting his own demons, so he moved to India to detox and travel on the yoga path in places like Rishikesh. We filmed him in the USA before he left and while he was in India. He's a very intelligent guy actually, really articulate, so the interviews are very enlightening, to use a pun. He is now back in the USA and fighting again. He recently came to Miami to see me. Then in 2015, we are scheduled to start shooting a documentary called *Danger Close* with a Special Forces veteran. This is a big departure from martial arts but the connection is that this Special Forces soldier is a weapons expert that combines his martial art training into his shooting technique, but I am not allowed to say any more than this. It is very intense to watch him move and shoot a gun. When we first met to discuss the movie he asked me if I am OK with loud bangs! We have been waiting four years for him to retire but he keeps getting asked to go back. He is on his way back from his last tour in Afghanistan at the moment and I hope to see him at Christmas.

KW: *How and where can people find your work?*

JB: On our website – www.emptymindfilms.com – you can download or rent our films. We also have a YouTube channel (www.youtube.com/user/emptymindfilms) or you can buy our documentaries through Amazon and a number of online distributors. Our programmes are also often on TV.

KW: *Thank you for your time and best of luck with* Warriors of Budo *and your other projects.*

45th Anniversary of Kendo in Buenos Aires, Argentina

By Gabriel Weitzner and Karina Cirone

Buenos Aires, Argentina, 1976. It was a late Friday afternoon, the sky was dark blue and it was raining heavily. This part of the city resembled East London. I arrived at the place I was looking for and was standing in front of a heavy looking double wooden door on Finochieto Street. Miyagi-sensei was at the door, and welcomed me by asking in broken Spanish, "What do you want?" I replied that I was looking for kendo practice; he invited me in.

For the very first time I saw folks wearing a blue *hakama* and *keikogi*. I didn't know what I was getting into, and in fact, I didn't really know what kendo was except for a recollection of a couple of Toshiro Mifune's movies, *Sanjuro* and *Yojimbo*.

Six months earlier

In March 1976, I enrolled in a Japanese conversation course at the Japanese Embassy. After a couple of months passed, a request was made for volunteers to assist the Japanese fencing team. They were to arrive soon after in order to participate in the Fencing World Championship, which was being held in Buenos Aires. The general request was to help the Japanese team, and to introduce them to Buenos Aires; a type of cultural exchange. I was a young university student delighted to help, and ready for an adventure.

In just a short time, I had built up a great rapport over food and drink with two Japanese fellows. They were Okusa-sensei, leader of the Japan Fencing Team, who was brilliant, open-minded and had a very sharp personality.

45th anniversary of the CKRA, AJA Taikai, October 2014

Miyagi-sensei at the 1988 WKC in Korea with Gabriel Oliva, Ernesto Kimura and Gabriel Weitzner

Kendo in AJA, 1978 - Kina, Borgarelli, Miyachi, Yamazaki, Cirone, Pascual and Weitzner

Unveiling of Miyagi-sensei's plaque and photo by his widow, Juana Miyagi

Argentina's first WKC in Sapporo 1979 - Carlos Pascual, Oscar Cirone and Ricardo Kina

Also, Mizukura Yuki, a very young Japanese student from Yokohama who was living in Buenos Aires for a six-month period. He was there to offer help to the Japanese team. We developed a friendship that we have nurtured since then; we are still in touch and see each other often in Japan and Canada. Okusa-sensei was also a kendoka and he passed on to me the address on Finochieto Street, where he insisted I go to get an introduction to kendo.

Kendo in Buenos Aires

Since 1954, Japanese immigrants that loved kendo got together at the Asociacion Japonesa Argentina (AJA); the group was named "Kendo Ai Ko Ka". The group disintegrated as its members slowly migrated and settled in the interior of Argentina, and *bōgu* and *shinai* were left at the AJA.

Miyagi Masakatsu-sensei arrived in Argentina in 1966, and like many Japanese at that time, he was looking for a new chapter in his life. He worked at AJA, and during the evenings he practised kendo on his own. Ernesto Kimura, a young fellow working at the Sei Nen Bu in the AJA, was intrigued by kendo and became the first kendo student there. Over time more people started kendo—in no particular order: Miyachi, Miura, Borgarelli, Ricardo Kina, Oscar Cirone, Carlos Pascual, and Sakae-sensei from JICA, among others.

As time passed by, Oscar Cirone and Carlos Pascual developed the opportunity to get visa sponsorship to Japan for kendo training, a project of several years. Because

Kasahara-sensei and Onuma-sensei at AJA, 1981

Nakata Yuji-sensei receiving the Facon Trophy from Admiral Oliva, the Argentine ambassador, in 1981

of that, Argentina was represented for the first time at the World Kendo Championships in Sapporo, 1979, by Oscar Cirone and Carlos Pascual. They continued to develop their skills in Japan for several years. Oscar Cirone returned to Argentina to share his experience, but Carlos Pascual remained in Japan under Kasahara-sensei's sponsorship.

Carlos Pascual had a remarkably productive experience in Japan, and, in conjunction with Admiral Gabriel Oliva, the Argentine Ambassador to Japan at that time, was able to present an Argentine Facon (a traditional silver gaucho knife) as a trophy to the All Japan Kendo Champion at the Nippon Budokan. The first of these trophies was presented to Nakata Yuji-sensei at the 1981 AJKC.

The Federation Argentina de Kendo (Argentine Kendo Federation (FAK)) was created in 1985 with Admiral Gabriel Oliva as its first president.

In 2010, the Confederacion de Kendo de la Republica Argentina was created with Oscar Cirone as its first president. The current president is Gustavo Adolfo Ramos.

In October 2014, kendo in Argentina celebrated its 45th Anniversary. The AJA is the cradle of kendo in Argentina, and due to the efforts, initiative, perseverance and personal sacrifice of Miyagi Masakatsu-sensei, kendo exists in Argentina today. On a personal note, I owe a lot to Miyagi-sensei. I took my first kendo steps thanks to his way of teaching. Even though I developed my kendo career in Canada, I always have in my heart the memory of Miyagi-sensei.

Unfortunately Miyagi Sensei passed away in 2001. To honour his memory, a plaque was unveiled by Miyagi-sensei's family at the AJA. Present at the ceremony were Mr. Hashimoto, secretary of the Japanese Embassy; Mr. Ikegaki, AJA's President; and Mr. Yamamoto from JICA. Also, as part of the 45th anniversary celebrations, a kendo competition was held with 150 participants from different kendo dojo from all over the country.

Currently the confederation has about 300 active members, and in early November they represented Argentina at the Atsugi 60th Anniversary Kendo Festival in Japan.

There have been many people who have contributed to the development of kendo in Argentina while showing persistence, perseverance and focus. Two notable people are Ernesto Kimura, who, as noted above, was Miyagi-sensei's first student, and over the years has helped to shape many students at AJA and helped to grow kendo in the Province of Mendoza; and Gustavo Ramos, who through his very hard work and personal sacrifice, helped to build a quite respectable kendo institution in the Province of Cordoba, among others.

On this, the 45th anniversary of kendo in Argentina, I wish that it will prosper into the future. To build great kendo for generations to come, one must never forget the past, history, and foundations. With that in mind, we should build new fundamentals on the experience of others, and always keep in mind what is the right thing to do in order to create a better future for kendo in Argentina.

Bujutsu Jargon Part 6

Reference guide covering various bujutsu-related terminology

Bruce Flanagan MA (Lecturer - Nanzan University)

#38 殺気 sakki

Sakki is the feeling of bloodthirsty emotion or focused concentration said to arise in an individual the moment before they attempt to kill someone. Various martial artists claim that they have trained their senses to detect *sakki* in a would-be assailant and teach students to respond in various ways when they sense *sakki* from a visible attacker or an attacker not in their field of view. *Sakki* differs from *satsui* (殺意), pre-meditated murderous intent.

#39 演武 enbu

A practice or display of martial arts or military exercises. In the purist sense, *enbu* refers to a demonstration of solo or paired forms as seen in *koryū* arts and not a display of free-sparring or point-scoring as seen in many modern *budō*, although its usage nowadays has become more relaxed. An *enbu-jō* (演武場) is the place where an *enbu* is performed which might be a specially-constructed venue or stage, a training or drill hall, or a parade ground or outdoor area. The *enbu-sha* (演武者) are the people who perform the *enbu*. Another similar word, *enbu* (演舞), means a practice or performance of dance.

#40 袈裟 kesa

Buddhist priests in China and Japan often wore a *kesa*, a decorative piece of cloth, as an outer garment over their robes. Although many sizes and designs exist, the *kesa* was generally wrapped around diagonally from the left shoulder down to the right hip. Due to the prevalence of this garment, sword cuts slashing down diagonally from the one shoulder to the opposite hip of an opponent came to be known as '*kesa*-cuts' (*kesa-giri* 袈裟斬り). Also, one of the *osae-waza* pinning techniques of judo is called the 'scarf hold' (*kesa-gatame* 袈裟固め).

#41 剣士 kenshi

A term for 'swordsman', 'fencer' or 'duellist'. There are a large number of terms for 'swordsman' including *kenjutsu-ka* (剣術家), *kenjutsu-tsukai* (剣術使い) and *kenkyaku* or *kenkaku* (剣客) among others. A prominent or master swordsman might be called a *kengō* (剣豪) and someone who was reputed to have achieved a superb level of technical and spiritual mastery in swordsmanship, such as Miyamoto Musashi, is often called *kensei* (剣聖) or 'sword saint'.

#42 礼儀作法 reigi-sahō

Reigi means 'etiquette' or 'courtesy' and *sahō* means 'manner' or 'method'. *Reigi-sahō* therefore means 'rules of etiquette'. Many methods of sitting, bowing, and walking, as well as rituals and ceremonies found in modern *budō* are generally governed by *reigi-sahō*. Many of these formalities find their roots in the Ogasawara-ryū school of etiquette which boasts a long history as the main instructors of etiquette to the shogunate (*bakufu*) and samurai houses (*buke*).

#43 無刀 mutō

Literally 'no-sword'. In the physical sense, *mutō* means that an individual is not armed with or wearing a sword. The term is also used to describe martial techniques in which an unarmed defender faces a sword-wielding attacker. Techniques in which the defender evades or stifles sword attacks and disarms their opponent are called *mutō-dori* (無刀取り). Among these *mutō-dori* is a special kind of technique called *shinken-shiraha-dori* (真剣白刃取り), or 'capturing a live sword blade', in which the defender directly grabs or traps the attacker's sword blade with their bare hands to disarm the attacker or turn the attacker's blade back on themselves. The nature of these techniques has been exaggerated by popular culture and *shinken-shiraha-dori* is now commonly understood as the act of stopping the movement of an overhead vertical sword cut by trapping the blade between the palms of both hands. For further reading on spiritual concepts of *mutō*, consult biographical information on Yagyū Munetoshi or the teachings of the Ittō Shōden Mutō-ryū founded by Yamaoka Tesshū.

#44 手裏剣 shuriken

Irrespective of size or design, a *shuriken* is a bladed throwing weapon. Although popularized in modern culture through 'ninja-stars', *shuriken-jutsu* was one of the 18 *bugei-jūhappan* warrior skills of the Edo period and even a *bushi* throwing his *wakizashi* at an enemy was technically a form of *shuriken-jutsu*. In their heyday, *shuriken* were usually heavy metal darts, nails, or spikes sharpened on one or both ends and were commonly called *bō-shuriken* (棒手裏剣) as opposed to the star-shaped *shaken* (車剣) of *ninjutsu* fame. In popular folklore the small and lightweight ninja-star's tips were usually coated in poison; however, the heavy *bō-shuriken* was designed to cause immediate injury and shock upon impact.

Bibliography
- *Bujutsu Jiten (Zusetsu)*, Osano J., Shinkigensha, 2003.
- *Kōjien (Daigohan)*, Iwanami Shoten, 2004.
- *Nichijōgo no naka no Budō Kotoba Gogen Jiten*, Katō H. & Nishimura R. (ed.), Tōkyōdō Shuppan, 1995.
- *Nihon Budō Jiten (Zusetsu)*, Sasama Y., Kashiwa-Shobō, 2003.

Review: *Kendo Playing Cards*

By Charlie Kondek

Surely you've seen some of your kendo friends on Facebook trying out Kendo Taikai, also known as Kendo Playing Cards (kendocards.com). I'm here to tell you this is an engaging, educational product for kendoka, and you should consider picking some up for you and your dojo. It would make an excellent gift for any kendoka you know, especially at its affordable price (see website for details).

Kendo Taikai is the invention of Akos Vachter, a Hungarian 4-dan who combined his interest in kendo and games to create a game that could be played by *kenshi* at the pub after *keiko*. That's exactly how we tested it at my dojo, and it was particularly welcome on a table crowded with pints and small plates, though it could of course flourish in any setting.

Kendo Taikai is a card game with a playing board that could be considered optional. The materials are of good quality and the illustrations on the cards are very good. Game play recreates a kendo match, with each player choosing from a set of brown or red *waza* cards and green "special" cards to assemble a hand that can then be played against the opponent. One plays an attack (brown) that can then be countered with combination *waza* or *ōji-waza* (red). The green special cards give particular abilities, such as the "Mushin" card, which you can play in response to any attack instead of having the appropriate counter card, or "Oshidashi", which allows you to push your opponent out of the *shiai-jō*, giving him *hansoku* (unless he can respond with the "Kaihi Suru" avoidance card!). There

are some attractive scoring counters to go with the board.

A couple of concerns with the game you should be aware of: the rules that come with it are printed in a tiny font and the language is a little unclear. For us Americans, the English translation was uneven. The best remedy for this is to go to the website and download the rules in a larger font (they are available in English, Japanese, French,

German, Italian, Spanish and Hungarian). Immerse yourself in the rules and spend time to understand them because they're a bit difficult to follow, particularly the special cards, which can only be used under certain circumstances. You'll want to test the game a few times to get the hang of it. Vachter recommends being as familiar as possible with the rules to take advantage of the game play. Each turn, you discard and pick up new cards, so a good player should be able to guess what's in play and what his opponent might spring on him. There are a few sample games in text and video at the web site.

The best part of the experience, for us, was that we could envision the match unfolding as represented by the cards in play on the table, and discuss the different situations they created – it really can be a continuation of *keiko* at the "second dojo." It was also a great tool for explaining *waza* and concepts to some of our newer members. What is "Seme"? What is "Fudoshin"? I can tell you that as the beer flowed and the hot wings were consumed, we engaged in much good-natured teasing and competitiveness.

I think these are early days for the game, and that Vachter may continue to evolve Kendo Taikai as he and more *kenshi* play it. This could lead to rules revisions, tournaments, new cards, special edition cards or other innovations. I hope you decide to give Kendo Taikai a try! We're going to keep playing it where I'm from.

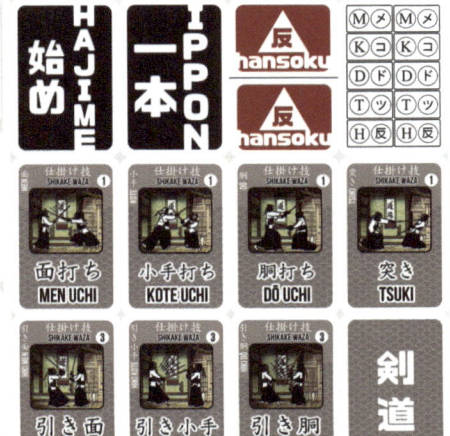

Two instructors from the Musashi Kai, Satō Futoshi, and Nakamura Tenshin during the April 2008 seminar in Salt Lake City.

The 7th U.S. Nitō Kendo Camp

By Robert Stroud

In July 2014, thanks in no small part to the generous support and participation of the Niten Ichi-ryū Musashi Kai (http://musashikai.jp/index.html), the annual U.S. Nitō Kendo Camp in Ontario, Oregon, was a great success. Over the last seven years a group of enthusiastic *kenshi* have gathered for this unique one-of-a-kind kendo seminar. The camp started in 2008 thanks to the efforts of Mike and Andria Wilkenson, who invited the Japan based Musashi Kai to participate in the April 2008 Nihon Matsuri Festival in Salt Lake City, Utah. That year the Musashi Kai was kind enough to send seven of its members, including Nakamura Tenshin, the chairman of their organisation. During that first visit the Musashi Kai gave public demonstrations, held introductory kendo clinics, and led U.S. *kenshi* in a *nitō*-focused seminar. For many of the *kenshi* attending it was their first exposure to the use of both swords as an extension of *ittō* kendo.

Following the camp in Salt Lake City several of the participants came away very motivated and were interested in finding a way to repeat the experience. Now, several years later, what started as a small idea to learn more about *nitō* has evolved into a dynamic, fun, and rewarding annual kendo camp. The event draws *kenshi* from across the U.S., Canada, Europe, and Latin America.

Lead instructors for the 2014 seminar were Sasaki Hirotsugi-sensei and Fujii Ryoichi-sensei, both K7-dan.

Sasaki-sensei is vice-chairman of the Niten Ichi-ryū Musashi Kai, coauthor of Musashi no Ken, and was a contributing author for the All Japan Kendo Federation's *Nitō Guidebook*. Fujii-sensei has been a long-time supporter of this camp and returned for his sixth visit this year. Two additional members of the Musashi Kai, 6-dan Ishimura Ako from Yamaguchi, and 4-dan Matsumoto Norikazu from Miyagi made the trip from Japan.

Because the Musashi Kai instructors have come to the U.S. multiple times, they have been able to provide a camp curriculum that builds upon past sessions, and teaches in a way that is both efficient and interesting for the participants. Each year's camp has included a great mix of new material and content that is suited for each attendee's level of kendo.

During the opening session this year, Sasaki-sensei pointed out that *nitō* has various reputations, but in his view it is just another perspective on kendo. For example, if you look at a bottle standing on a table, you could say "this is kendo". However, if you pick it up and look at it from one of its ends, you might not think you are still looking at kendo—but you are, just from a different point of view. Since seeing things from a different perspective is useful, you can expand your understanding and improve all aspects of your kendo including *ittō* when you study *nitō*.

Musashi Kai sensei Satō Futoshi, and Fujii Ryoichi demonstrate nitō vs. nitō keiko during the April 2008 seminar in Salt Lake City.

In Miyamoto Musashi's writings he maintained that in combat there are instances when you need to wield a sword with one hand. For example, when one arm has been injured or cut, you should know how to continue fighting with either hand in order to protect yourself. The same holds true about footwork and you should be able to fight using various kinds. A principle presented during the camp as an extension of the above point is that if two swords are carried, then two swords can be used.

Drills in footwork started with an introduction to *namba-ashi*, the old "samurai way" of walking, which can be thought of as "bear style". Instead of your opposite arm swinging forward with your step as in modern walking, *namba-ashi* is done with the arm and leg of the same side moving forward with each step. *Namba-ashi* is useful for walking through difficult conditions like mud or ice.

Samurai probably employed this walking style to keep their hips squared, stance stable, and perhaps keep their swords from swaying side to side while walking. This use of hip and body coordination, and its use as a base for proper execution of *nitō* (and *ittō*) techniques, was covered in some depth during the camp. By moving and keeping the hips square to the opponent, your strikes will have a solid foundation. This will improve your *hikitsuke* (pulling in the trailing leg) so that you will be able to reach your target without leaning forward and then strike again as needed. This is because your hips are under your torso and you will have better balance.

As in past years, the Nippon Kendo Kata was used to illustrate common concepts that are important to *nitō* and *ittō* kendo. In *ippon-me*, the concept of *maai* is key, and therefore the *maai* must be determined as you judge the distance without the sword tips touching. In *nihon-me*,

Group picture from the first U.S. Nitō Camp, April 2008 in Salt Lake City.

the concept of using the centreline is shown by *shidachi* moving to the side of the incoming attacking plane and forming a new plane. *Sanbon-me* illustrates *datotsu-kikai* (striking opportunities): after *uchidachi*'s first attack is finished; when *uchidachi* is about to attack again; and finally when *uchidachi* stops, tries to retreat, and *shidachi* chases him down. The use of the Nippon Kendo Kata to illustrate how to properly interact with one's opponent helped the experienced participants in refining their overall kendo skills, and allowed newer students to start their study of *nitō* from a strong, familiar foundation.

Another concept covered in the camp was the use of "*jūshin*", or the centre of gravity of an object. The *shinai*'s centre of gravity is key to swinging it effectively. This is also the key to striking quickly and with sufficient "snap" for small *men* in *ittō*, and one-handed *katate* strikes in both *ittō* and *nitō* kendo. Sasaki-sensei discussed this point: If you cut with either hand dominant, the centre of rotation will be located on the *tsuka*, which requires extra strength and coordination to compensate for the imbalance. To make a sharp strike (*sae*), especially with one hand, you only need to rotate the blade around its centre and let gravity swing the sword. It should not be about muscle power. Much time was spent covering the use of the *shinai*'s centre of gravity as a key point during *seme* to engage an *aite*.

In addition to the discussion of the finer points mentioned above, time was spent in drills that supported each point in kata, *waza*, and properly making strikes. As the camp unfolded, more advanced topics were presented, including the 13 Nitō Kendo Kata, how to apply the concepts to two *shinai*, and strategies for *ittō* facing *nitō*, *ittō* facing *jōdan*, etc.

Besides the three full days of kendo lectures and drills, there was also a daily *gōdō-geiko*, where people were able to try their new *shiai* skills against the Musashi Kai members and with each other. On Sunday, the annual red vs. white *taikai* was a chance for everyone to try both *ittō* and *nitō* kendo in a *shiai* setting. Half of the camp made up the red team and the other half the white, with the sensei as *shinpan*. In the first round the red side all used *nitō* against the white, who did *ittō*. In the second round the red and white teams switched styles. It was a great match with spirited competition, and served as a great ending to a wonderful kendo camp.

When not training together the camp participants were able to muster up enough energy to sample local food and beverages. This included stops at a microbrew pub, an authentic Méxican restaurant, and lively bidding during the *sayanora* party and auction. The enthusiasm continued until late each night with people comparing notes, talking about the day's lesson, and just finding time to have some fun with kendo friends new and old.

Plans are already underway for the 2015 camp. It will be returning to Ontario, Oregon, and is scheduled for the weekend of June 26-28. Camp organisers are looking forward to seeing returning participants, and are extending a welcome to those who will be attending for the first time. More information about the 2015 camp can be found here: http://www.idaho-kendo.com/nito/

常識を超える
勝利のゴールドマーク

ALL JAPAN BUDOGU
FREE INTERNATIONAL SHIPPING ON ALL ORDERS!

www.alljapanbudogu.com

On set of Robin Hood *with Richard Greene*

From an Introduction to Kendo

'A MAN OF MANY PARTS'
Portrait of an Inimitable Swordsman
Ronald Alexander Lidstone (1895—1969)

Part 2: The Old Vic, Robin Hood, and Rashomon

By Paul Budden

Kendo as a sport had been attracting popular attention, but unfortunately, when war broke out, this put paid to any immediate future development. Okamoto and Kudzutani-sensei, who had both been staunch supporters of the Anglo Japanese Judo Club, returned to Japan. The consequence of this was that kendo nearly died out, except for spasmodic sessions and demonstrations given by R.A. Lidstone and Nakano Hidetake, a 2-dan who, like Mishiku Kaoru-sensei, remained in Britain rather than return to Japan.

Mishiku-sensei was taken by the British military to Hereford and instructed to teach unarmed combat (judo/jujutsu) to the British forces. He refused, stating that although it was his choice to remain, he could not teach British soldiers how to kill Japanese soldiers. The military hierarchy persisted in their requests, but Mishiku-sensei kept refusing and after a short while he was released and reunited with his wife. He was not interned for the rest of the war. According to his wife, if anybody asked about their nationality, they said they were Chinese to avoid any confrontation.

Following the war years, Mishiku-sensei worked very hard to rebuild the club that had moved to Sandycombe Road, Kew, London. Kendo resumed there, so did some of the other judo clubs, but it lacked any real structure. Most of the time it was just the judo practitioners putting on some kendo armour to have an informal bash. Renowned judo teacher and former member of the Jubilee (Ōtani Masutarō's judo club) Bill Stopps said the following:

"I had started kendo and bought a couple of kits from Harry Johnson, paying 4 pounds, and used to train in Wornington Road, Kensington (probably the Evening Institute around Gorborne Road), but after a while

Mishiku-sensei, Anglo Japanese Judo Club

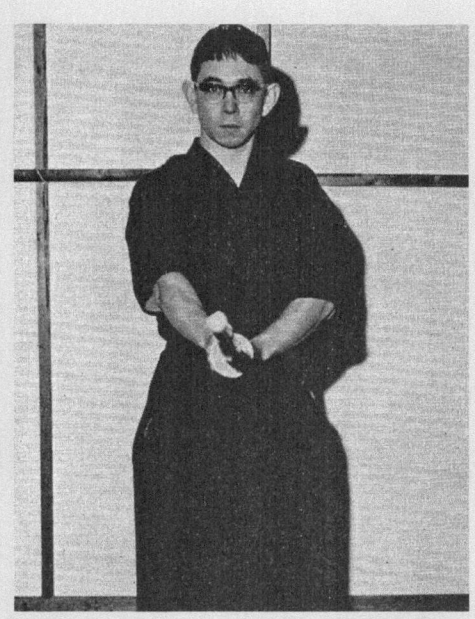
Ōtani Tomio – The Japanese Fighting Arts

the kendo got boring and I used to get headaches. So I sold the kits to a fellow at the Ealing Club, in Bond Street (now gone) for 4 pounds. On the side of the breastplate there was some Japanese writing. I met the fellow sometime later, he told me that a Japanese had come up to him and said that the breastplates had his name on them and that they belonged to him – he had left them at the Anglo Japanese Judo Club before leaving the country (presumably at the outbreak of the war). Anyway the Japanese grabbed the kits and marched off".[1]

This loose tradition continued until Ōtani Tomio (the eldest son of judo master Ōtani Masutarō), who came to Britain in 1919, began to practise kendo on a daily basis with martial arts instructor Abe Kenshirō, who had arrived in England in 1955. Throughout the 1960s, Ōtani-sensei was to offer an alternative kendo organisation to the emerging British Kendo Association (circa 1964), the "British Kendo Council". He opened the first "kendo only" dojo, the Acton Kendo Kyushinkan, in north London in 1961. He ran three clubs in London and provided information on kendo through articles in various publications. One of these was in the book *The Japanese Fighting Arts* (1966), edited by John Goodbody [2] with photographs by Brendan Monks. His article was written when kendo in Britain was still floundering in its infancy, and demonstrates the depth of his understanding of kendo, and includes clear explanations of both technical terms and kendo philosophy.

Following the end of the war, R.A. did very little kendo for nearly 15 years, apart from giving the odd demonstration. This was due mainly to a very heavy workload from his many appointments as a fight director. He was starting to make a name for himself as a stage and film fight choreographer, as well as teaching fencing and acrobatics at the Old Vic and the Central School for Speech and Drama. He also had contracts with both film and TV, and was also a founding member of the Society of British Fight Directors. This busy routine, coupled with changes of location around the country, made it difficult to maintain any regular kendo practice. However, introducing elements of kendo when working out fight routines for the varied productions added to his already extensive knowledge of sword-play and sword fighting.

Brian, his youngest son, recollected that at times he assisted in the preparation of various fight routines. He played the parts of Errol Flynn, Robert Taylor, and Richard Greene, amongst other notable actors and performers, while his father worked on the often complicated sequences.

R.A. re-started kendo on a full-time basis only in the late 1950s after exchanging letters and meeting with Roald Knutsen. Knutsen had discovered three sets of kendo armour at the London Judo Society in Vauxhall in 1957, and began to practise kendo. A document written by R.A., a precursor to his book *An Introduction to Kendo*, was lent to Knutsen by a colleague, Harry Russell Robinson, at the Tower of London Armouries where he was studying. Robinson introduced Lidstone to Knutsen, who would

Directing Errol Flynn

Film poster for The Dark Avenger, 1955

later assist in the publication of the book with technical advice and drawings.

This document, together with two small booklets in Japanese, formed Knutsen's early basis for learning. However, his initial interest in kendo had been sparked by F.J. Norman's book *The Fighting Man of Japan: The Training and Exercises of the Samurai* (1905) [3], which he had read when he was just 14. Knutsen then met R.A. in 1958 at the London Judo Society. Then, at the informal Shinto Ryu Kendo Club, they started to practise kendo together, officially joining the Shinto Ryu Club in 1959. R.A. later became an instructor and vice-president of the club.

Through the persistent efforts of Roald Knutsen, his wife Patricia, R.A. and others including Dr. Benjamin H. Hazard in America, the British Kendo Association (BKA) was established in 1962. It was officially registered in 1964 with R.A. appointed as its first chairman. The BKA received a high level of support from the All Japan Kendo Federation (AJKF), which started through correspondence with a group of *sensei* headed by H9-dan Ozawa Takashi, K8-dan Arai Shigeo, and H8-dan Takizawa Kōzō, who later became vice-president of the BKA. The Japanese Embassy in London also assisted. The statutes for the Oshu Kendo Renmei, the forerunner to the European Kendo Federation, were also formulated in 1966. Roald Knutsen started the Nenriki Kendo Club in Elephant and Castle, London in the same year.

Nenriki Kendo Club, named by Dr. Itō Kyoitsu and endorsed by the AJKF (the new authority for kendo in Japan), was officially opened in 1967. Among the sixty or so guests who attended the opening were Sir Frank and Lady Bowden, and Captain Yoshimura Gorō, the Japanese Naval Attaché in London. R.A. acted as master of ceremonies. Osaki Shintarō, a student of Dr. Itō Kyoitsu and a prominent figure in the AJKF, arrived in England. He stayed with the Knutsen family whilst studying at college, and added greatly to the development of the BKA.

Prominent Japanese kendo teachers made official and private visits to London, and some of them remained in Britain. The first meeting of the Oshu Kendo Renmei took place in Brussels, to confirm the status of the association, in January of the same year.

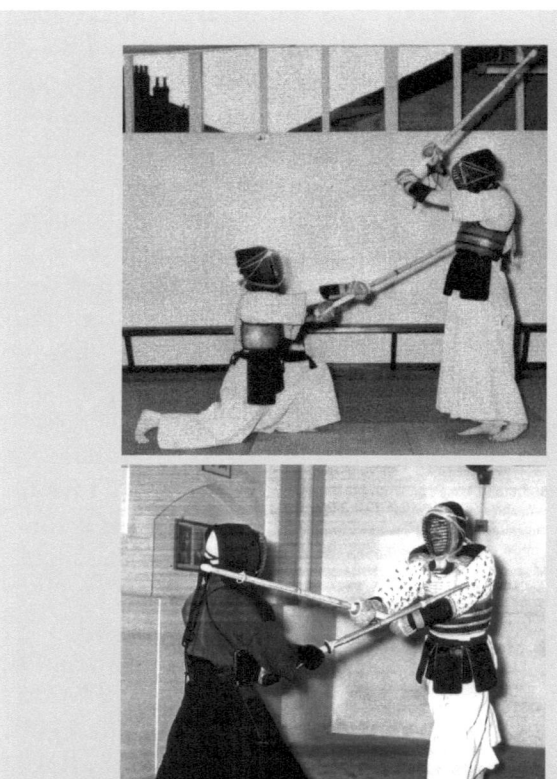
Shinto Ryu dojo, Kennington

Takizawa Kōzō-sensei

Shinto Ryu dojo, Kennington

Sir Frank Bowden, who was greatly interested in Japan, became a future president of the BKA and a vice-president of the Japan Society. In 2000 he was awarded the "Order of the Rising Sun with Golden Rays and Rosette" by the Emperor of Japan.

At times, R.A. paid visits to the various dojo in the southern counties to teach and leave behind some of his boundless enthusiasm, which helped greatly in increasing the membership of the BKA. He wrote an article on kendo for The Fencing Master and gave talks, a notable one being for the Anglo-Japanese Society of London at the Victoria and Albert Museum in 1962.

In 1963 he was called in to direct the fighting in a stage version of the renowned Japanese film Rashomon at the Citizen's Theatre in Glasgow. On January 30, 1964, he wrote to his daughter Joan, "I have been asked to go to Manchester, to the Library Theatre, to show them how to handle a Japanese sword."

From 1967 to 1969, prominent sensei from Japan, including senior officials of the AJKF, visited Britain. These included Ozawa Takashi, Matsumoto Toshio, Izawa Zensaku, Hirano Soyao, Takizawa Kōzō, and Ohtaki Gorō. Part of R.A.'s duty as chairman was to host the small parties of visitors for sightseeing and to ensure they were suitably accommodated, watered and fed. These were often punishing schedules, and each day left him undoubtedly exhausted, but he felt exhilarated being with such important and interesting people. On one such occasion, after saying his final farewells to the visitors in Regent Street, the party broke into spontaneous clapping as he walked off in appreciation of his efforts to make their visit the success that it had been.

As a tribute to his endeavours over so many years in fostering a lasting interest in kendo in the United Kingdom,

With Ozawa Takashi-sensei and Osaki Shintarō-sensei in front of Buckingham Palace

not least for his book on the subject, the AJKF awarded him the title of Renshi; the only other European raised to this status at the time was, coincidentally, Roald Knutsen.

The text on the menjō reads:

"R. A. Lidstone is hereby appointed Kendo Renshi on January 10, 1970, by the All Japan Kendo Federation. (Signed) Kimura Tokutarō, Chairman"

Realising there was no book on kendo in English, R.A. completed his treatise, *An Introduction to Kendo*. There is evidence that the project began in the 1930s, but it turned out to be a labour of love, carried out over many years, as it was not completed and published until 1964 [4]. His patient persistence in the task of writing such a book, coupled with his determination to master Japanese kendo terminology translated into English, brought forth a work that, although now sadly out of print, is still regarded as a pioneer work of great importance.

Lidstone's Renshi menjō

An Introduction to Kendo

R.A. Lidstone from *An Introduction to Kendo*

Brian Lidstone, R.A's youngest son, presenting the same two shinai (left photo) to the author

In a letter to R.A.'s eldest son David, B.W. Robinson, Deputy Keeper of Metallurgy at the Victoria and Albert Museum, London, and one of the foremost authorities on Japanese swords outside of Japan in the 1960s, wrote:

"I greatly admired his enthusiasm and skill in both European fencing and kendo. I know it was a satisfaction to him to see the latter firmly established in England since the war, after he had been virtually the sole exponent in this country for so long. He was indeed, the patriarch – though a most lively one – of the art so far as England was concerned, a position well established by his excellent book on the subject (of which I am proud to own a copy inscribed to me by him). He will be greatly and widely missed."

On his death, his valuable collection of fencing books from his personal library was donated by the family to the Tower of London Library, which has since been moved to Leeds, where they were starting a new sports section.

R.A. Lidstone achieved the grades of 6-kyū in 1936, 2-dan in 1962 and 4-dan in 1967. Unfortunately, his Renshi title, which was to have been conferred in Japan, had to be made posthumously in 1970 following his untimely death on October 10, 1969, whilst practising at Nenriki Kendo Club in London.

Always energetic and keen on fitness, he had a fear that either through illness or old age he would lose his mental capacities. Perhaps when he suddenly collapsed and died, the end was as he would have preferred it. A memorial competition has been held annually at Nenriki since that time in commemoration of this remarkable man and in recognition of a lifetime's contribution to British kendo.

A man who exemplified an ideal to live up to, he was inspirational in strength of mind and a knight to courtesy. He rests with his beloved Isolde in Bray cemetery near Windsor.

R.A. Lidstone Biography

Books:
Studies in Symbology. (1926)
   The Symbology of the Crucifix & the Tarot
   Symbology & the Types of Man
   Symbology of the initiations & the Tarot
   Symbology of the Number 12

The Art of Fencing: A Practical Manual for Foil Epee and Sabre (1930)
Bloody Bayonets: The Complete Guide to Bayonet Fighting (1942)
Fencing: A Practical Treatise on Foil, Epee, Sabre (1952)
An Introduction to Kendo: R.A.Lidstone (Charles Alexis) (1964)
Castle, Egerton. (Lidstone, R.A. ed. and Foreword) *Schools and Masters of Fencing: From the Middle Ages to the Eighteenth Century 3rd Edition*, Arms and Armour, London. 1969.

Filmography:
1925. *Rewi's Last Stand*—Fight Director
1953. *Knights of the Round Table.* Starring Robert Taylor & Ava Gardner—Fight Director
1954. *Men of Sherwood Forest.* Starring Don Taylor—Fight Director
1955. *The Dark Avenger.* Starring Errol Flynn—Fight Director

Acting:
1925. Rewi's Last Stand—Von Tempskey

Television:
1956–57. *The Adventures of Sir Lancelot.* Starring William Russell.—Master At Arms
1955 -59. *Robin Hood.* Starring Richard Greene - Fight Director
1959. *ITV Play of the Week*—Stunt arranger
1963. *As You Like It*—Wrestling coordinator

Theatre:
1949–1963. The Old Vic, Sadler's Wells, Covent Garden, Citizen's Theatre Glasgow, Saville Theatre—Fight Director

1969. Founder member of the Society of British Fight Directors

Dance:
1919–36. The professional "Adagio" dance duo "Isolde and Alexis" and musical act "Isolde Alexis and Carlo" performances *Notwithstanding* at the Café de Paris in London, the London Coliseum and a tour of South Africa in 1923, the BBC *Midday Musical Hall*.

REFERENCES AND BACKGROUND SOURCES
'Ronald' & 'Isolde' books compiled and written by David Lidstone and Joan Childs (Nee Lidstone)
The Alexander Turnbull Library New Zealand
John Bowen, the personal records of his late brother Richard Bowen 'Judo history'
The British Newspaper Archive
The Budokwai 'Judo History Records'
British Pathe
Roald and Pat Knutsen, personal records
The National Library of New Zealand and Papers Past
Frank Perry and the 'Bu'sen Martial Arts School, London
Wikipedia

ACKNOWLEDGEMENTS
I would like to thank Brian Lidstone, his wife Jenny, and members of the Lidstone Family, Roald and Pat Knutsen, John Bowen, Kazuyo Matsuda, Terry Holt, Ian Parker Dodd, and Frank Perry for their invaluable information, generous assistance, and great kindness.

Endnotes
1. Bill Stopps was a renowned judo teacher and the first personal assistant to judo master Ōtani Masutarō from 1947. The quote is from the "Judo Forum" and is based on a rough transcript from a tape received by the British Judo Council from Bill Stopps in July 1993. http://judo.forumsmotion.com/t747-bill-stopps-talks-about-otani-abe-and-others
2. John Goodbody was for many years chief sports writer for *The Times* and has covered every Olympics since 1964. The publication quoted is *The Japanese Fighting Arts* (1967), printed by the Garden City Press Ltd, Letchworth Herts. Library of Congress Catalogue Number: 69-12801. Brendan Monks is a photographer and sports picture editor at the *Daily Mail*.
3. Norman, F.J. *The Fighting Man of Japan: The Training and Exercises of the Samurai* (Foreword by Alexander Bennett), Bunkasha International, Chiba. Reissued in 2003.
4. In the *Bloody Bayonets* (1942) title listings page, Squadron Leader R.A. Lidstone is noted as the author of *Kendo: The Art of Japanese Swordsmanship*. This implies that a preliminary version under a different title had been produced before 1940 and possibly as early as 1936. This is also indicated in the Lidstone personal archive notes. To date we have not been able to trace any copies of this publication.

LIDSTONE KYŪSHA MEMORIAL TAIKAI
London, England

By Alexander Thomas
Photos courtesy of Errol Blake, Paul Budden and Debbie Bevan

I have always been what some may call a "slow learner" when it comes to many things, and kendo is no exception. Despite several injuries that forced my time spent training to become erratic and unfocused, I managed to attain the rank of 4-kyu within my dojo. This spurred me on to train more and harder, but a sickness that followed cut that notion short.

For a while I was looking for a reason to continue studying kendo. My mentors and dojo mates are helpful and pushed me to succeed, but due to a visual disability and a few recurring illnesses, the cause of which did not come to light until recently, I felt that my performances had been patchy at best.

While browsing the British Kendo Association website, I found an advertisement for a beginner-orientated *taikai* being held in London, just an hour's train ride away. This interested me, as the majority of competitions in my area are usually aimed towards more advanced kendoka. I signed up to participate before I had even finished reading the full advertisement and details. At the time, I was not sure why I was so quick to sign up, as my training had been sporadic, but realised why when I turned up at the event.

Many people made their way to the near secluded sports hall just outside Waterloo Station, London. It was obvious from the start that the attending kendoka had differing levels of skill and knowledge, which made me feel like a first time beginner all over again.

The morning started with a small and less formal introduction to the Lidstone Taikai and what it is about. Its focus is on the newer, maybe less experienced members of the kendo community, and introduces them to the rules, etiquette and structure of a *taikai*. One thing I became aware of from the start is that the Lidstone Taikai has a lot of tradition and history behind it, though it is kept easily accessible for newer kendoka.

Following the warm and friendly opening speech, everyone was divided into groups so they could start practising for the main competition. There were small bouts with only one referee in quick rotation for over an hour, which was a good warm up, and at one point I became aware that my cardio and endurance is not as good as I thought. The smaller practice fights were a good entry for someone who has never been in a refereed match before, especially when the official presiding over you would stop the bout and tell you what you were doing right and wrong and how to correct your mistakes.

After a break for lunch we moved on to the *taikai* proper, which started with a speech about the history of the competition, which can be found on the Lidstone Memorial Taikai website. Further explanations of scoring, who wears what colours and why, and the full rules of the competition were given. Since this was a competition for people under *shodan*, *tsuki* techniques were not permitted.

On a personal note, I told myself before the *taikai*, "I don't mind if I lose, as long as I don't embarrass myself, for me this is a learning experience". So in my preliminary fight, my first-ever scored competition, I turned up to fight without my *kote* on! Luckily I managed to redeem myself by winning my preliminary bouts before being knocked out by the eventual winner.

In my second match my opponent landed a point early and that shook me a bit. Despite being good defensively, my offense crumbled after several attempts to land an *ippon* – none of my strikes were getting through. After a few minutes my footwork fell apart to the point where I was leaping into strikes to try and increase their speed. After the fight I shook hands with my opponent knowing that I had found what I was looking for and why I signed up to the *taikai*.

I needed to know where I was going wrong, and I needed someone to face, and to be beaten by someone outside of my dojo, where I had become far too comfortable with my own ability. That does not mean that my teachers and dojo mates do not push me and help me all they can, because they do. However, I needed to see where I was going wrong, and what holes I needed to fill from a totally different perspective.

The Lidstone Taikai organisers and staff were friendly and accommodating, even taking my disability into consideration as much as they could. The *taikai* was more than reasonably priced for entry, the location very

The author (right) in action

handy, and the information and preparation provided were spectacular. I would just like to take a moment to again thank the organisers, staff and participants of the 2013 Lidstone Taikai.

To sum up, going to a competition for the first time was one of the best things I could have done for my kendo. Based on my experiences, I would suggest a few things for anyone attending a *taikai* or similar event for the first time. Take your time, and ask questions if you need to. The rules and etiquette will be slightly different from what you do at your dojo. It may be easy to feel intimidated being around kendo dignitaries and far more experienced kendoka, but just remember, people who have been there and done it before want to help you into the broader community, not push you away.

There are also many reasons why you should go to a *taikai*, or even a larger training seminar. You may learn things that you have not picked up in your daily or weekly training. You will also pick up more from the practical application of everything you have learned; you will have the chance to get rid of that "stage fright", performing in front of a large group of people with officials overseeing what you are doing; and, you will quickly find that any fear or doubts you had will turn into determination.

More information on the Lidstone Taikai can be found here: http://lidstonetaikai.blogspot.co.uk/

World Kendo Network

By Donatella Castelli

Held during Golden Week in Kyoto in early May, the Kyoto Enbu Taikai is like a kendo festival. There are many *keiko-kai* and parties held throughout Kyoto and it attracts kendoka from not only all around Japan, but also from around the world. This year, and for the second time, the WKN had a set of events - two *keiko-kai*, a friendly competition, and a party.

"WKN" stands for "World Kendo Network", and before telling the all-too-short, but surprisingly dynamic history of the largest kendo related Facebook group with more than 10,000 members, a definition of it would be in order. However, it seems better to define what WKN is not.

WKN is not:

— a club or a federation. It has no intention to be an alternative to the traditional and well established structures that organise (nationally or internationally) all official kendo activities. On the contrary, the ambition of the WKN is to give to all official kendo organisations a further method of communication with the rest of the world by acting as a well-connected sounding board.

— a commercial endeavour. There are no application forms or membership fees. On the WKN Facebook wall, members can publicise and sell items related to martial arts and, to a certain degree, Japanese art; are encouraged to share their experiences, in the form of words and images; are urged to pool their information to further spread the reach of the WKN.

— a "school" of Kendo. Although high ranked sensei take part in WKN events and share their kendo wisdom on the Facebook wall, the purpose is not to establish a school with a traditional hierarchy. The WKN offers the opportunity to establish direct contact between students (or potential students) and teachers, wherever they may be based.

To define the WKN in the positive, it is an original contribution to the kendo community that utilises the internet and social networks, and its purpose is *keiko*. The WKN shares information that leads to *keiko*, real encounters and real friendship.

"Network" is the keyword, making people communicate, exchange ideas, trade information, meet and practise together. The social aspect of kendo has always existed, of course, but the WKN would like to make it central, in order to reach larger numbers of people, be they budo enthusiasts, Japanophiles or hard-core kenshi.

The idea behind the WKN is the absolute faith that kendo embodies values worth spreading, not only to facilitate human relations, but also to ultimately achieve the goal of world peace. Too ambitious? Maybe, but the ambition of doing something universally good has never been considered hubris. After all, every kenshi knows that the "Purpose of Practising Kendo", as established by the All Japan Kendo Federation (AJKF), includes two seemingly very abstract goals:

> To contribute to the development of culture And to promote peace and prosperity among all peoples

The WKN would like to offer help to those who consider these goals as important as making a correct *men-uchi* or performing a powerful *fumikiri*.

The first target of the WKN is to reach one-million members by having them joining the Facebook group. From there, the WKN will provide them with a reliable means of communication that would support and encourage people to take part in kendo, to meet, to practise together and to spread through practice the values that the Facebook wall purports.

A Bit of History (after all, there is only a bit...)

The World Kendo Network was born in May 2012, in Kyoto, around a dinner table. Eight very different people, all kenshi, met without even knowing where the adventure would lead them, or even if the new-born WKN would have a chance to live on. The first event that mixed art performances (dance, music and belcanto) and *keiko*, with demonstrations of rare *kata*, and a "Japan vs. Rest of the World" *shiai*, took place in May 2013. There were around 30 participants, but the friendly and collaborative atmosphere was very encouraging.

18 months later, thanks to a lot of work not only by the WKN's founding fathers and mothers, the group now has more than 11,000 members and is continuing to grow. The obscure currents of Facebook are difficult to understand, but waves of South American kenshi followed a tsunami of European members, while members in North America and Oceania keep growing steadily. The WKN is slowly spreading throughout Asia, too, and to encourage Japanese kenshi to join, a Japanese language Facebook group has been created - language barriers are even harder to break out of the dojo.

The WKN's Present Status

Can kendo (and budo in general) count on a million passionate aficionados that are all willing to keep in touch and practise together whenever they have a chance? That dream seems within reach. WKN members have started to be empowered to create their own WKN gatherings or to participate in official events under the WKN's collective name. This ideal is slowly turning into a reality. *Keiko* around the world is possible, and the WKN hopes to open the doors of all dojo in the world to kenshi who wish to wholeheartedly have *keiko* with like-minded kenshi near their home or while on a trip, where access is made difficult through language barriers or local habits.

The Next Steps?

First of all, the aim to create a calendar of WKN events in each continent and to create local contacts to make "globalisation" a clean and happy word.

Second, to create some kind of a structure in each country by finding WKN "editors" who would like to keep the pages alive with local events, photos, reports. Facebook is an extraordinary tool, but the purpose of WKN is to turn the virtual into real, so real kenshi are the key to keep the flame alive.

Final Thoughts

The World Kendo Network's founders firmly believe that kendo and budo are valid means to achieve world peace, because even though the kendo world may be small, it is full of great people. So, *ganbarimashō* and let's keep counting!

Wish to Know More?
Join our Facebook group!

The WKN administrators are Maruyama Kōichi (Japan), Simon Conlin (Canada), and Donatella Castelli (Italy / the Netherlands / Japan).

A STRANGER IN [KENDO] PARADISE

By Alan Stephenson (R6-dan)

The New Zealand Kendo Federation has approximately 300 members at present. Like most organisations that are purely voluntary, there is a small but serious group who run kendo in New Zealand and who devote their lives to the maintenance and growth of this wonderful martial art. As well as being a small organisation, we are well spread out throughout the country, which means that we practise with the same people most of the time in our local dojo. Also, in my experience, the reality for most non-Japanese kendo practitioners who live in another country is that we tend to visit Japan for short kendo stints of one or two weeks for events like the Foreign Kendo Leaders' Summer Seminar in Kitamoto or the Kyoto Taikai, to name but a few.

As a person who practises and loves kendo, but who lives outside Japan, it has always been a dream of mine to spend a significant amount of time in that country where the depth and breadth of kendo is obviously far greater than that in New Zealand. For the last 15 to 20 years, the kendo situation in New Zealand has led me to want to stay and practise kendo in Japan to widen my experience and knowledge. However, due to work commitments and a whole raft of other complexities, I have had to live with only the dream and not the reality. As a consequence of this constant yearning to be in Japan, and the combination of several other factors that occurred in my life over the last couple of years, I decided to take the plunge and ask my new boss, who is an enlightened and broad-minded person, for four months leave of absence to undertake "a period of learning in Japan". It was with great delight, and a bit of a surprise, that he agreed to my request as long as I worked out the details of my replacement. Excitedly, my wife Naoko and I went about organising a four-month visit to Japan from April to August, 2014.

When fellow Kiwi Dr. Alex Bennett, in his role as Editor-in-Chief of Kendo World, requested that I write an article on a memorable topic or event for me since my arrival in Japan in April, I agreed. However, in truth it has been a bit of a struggle for me to isolate one event out of all of the great experiences I have had to date, not to mention the very warm hospitality that has so far been afforded to Naoko and myself by everyone we have met since arriving.

After a day or so of reflection, my thinking turned to the All Japan Kendo Enbu Taikai (commonly known as the "Kyoto Taikai"), held every year in May at the Butokuden in Kyoto. If you can only attend one event in Japan, I definitely recommend that this be the one; if at all possible, participate in it as well. This was my second time taking part in the kendo matches, and I also had the opportunity to feast my eyes on the incredible demonstrations of jodo and iaido by literally a thousand or so practitioners. Whilst the length of a kendo *enbu* is only 90 seconds, there is a lot of learning that takes place in that short space of time, the benefits of which have been immeasurable.

Another of my highlights from the *enbu* involved watching the clash of the kendo titans, world-famous sensei who have been to NZ before, as well as a host of other famous and talented kendoka who put on great displays of skill that enthralled and captivated the audience. For a person like me who does not get this type of exposure on a regular basis, it was like being a stranger in kendo paradise.

While the *taikai* is on, there is also the opportunity for kendoka to attend *asa-geiko* (morning practice) – the most incredible scene to watch. The attending 8-dan sensei line up in two rows, back to back down the centre of the hall and all the 6-dan and 7-dan participants form rows of approximately eight to 10 people deep around the perimeter walls of the Budo Centre, patiently waiting for their turn to practise with the best of the best. I was fortunate enough to practice with six 8-dan sensei during the two sessions I attended, which is equivalent to, under ordinary circumstances in New Zealand, about three years of practise with visiting sensei of that level.

Another great memory was the opportunity to catch up with international kendo friends that were also there. Normally I would only get the opportunity to meet them at events like the World Kendo Championships (held every three years). I also had the opportunity to make some new friends. It was a pleasure for me to meet some of the high fliers in iaido and jodo from the UK and Europe whose names I knew but whom I had never met.

I should also mention that there is an opportunity to go about purchasing budo-related items that are on sale by the many companies that attend the event to specifically take advantage of the huge number of budoka who are present. Anything you might need or want for your budo pursuits is available, either there on the spot or to order.

The main things that I have experienced, observed, and learnt during my opportunities to practise with Japanese kendo practitioners so far (versus my usual situation of practising with non-Japanese in New Zealand) is that for the most part, Japanese start kendo at a much younger age than the average Kiwi. Even though I feel our basics in New Zealand are very sound and correct, starting kendo at a much younger age means generally that the Japanese have superior muscle memory built into their kendo. This manifests itself in what can be a difficult thing to put your finger on. However, I am going to express it as preparedness and the timing of a cut or strike in *keiko*.

I have found that the difference between Japanese timing and what I am more accustomed to in New Zealand is very tangible. When I attempt a strike that is sometimes at the incorrect time, and when not optimally prepared, my opponent simply blocks or deflects my cut, as they are perfectly settled and can receive an ill-timed cut.

There is also the situation where my attempt at a cut is not as efficient as theirs, and when we both launch for a strike, I am beaten to the target area. This, I believe, is a situation where my Japanese partner's *seme* is superior to mine, and is accompanied by an ability to produce techniques with cleaner lines and more economical movement. Importantly, this means that they land their strike a fraction of a second earlier.

For me, kendo is a unique feeling or emotion-based meta-physical pursuit. Sometimes we find it difficult to express or articulate what is happening in the process of an engagement, and who is actually on top at any particular point in time during the fight. However, we all know the common feelings we have while practising kendo. Our gut feeling tells us when our partner is in control in the fight, or when we are in control, even though from the outside this may not be evident to the observer. These subtleties are the hallmarks of the profoundly deep art that is kendo. One thing is certain: It is crucial to honestly and consistently keep working on honing one's skills, as well as economising movement and effort through repeated practising of *waza*. This way we can learn, on an ongoing basis, how to squeeze the most out of ourselves.

There is no end to this though, and there is no line in the sand that tells us when we have got there. It is an almost unobtainable goal, as the line keeps moving away from us as we strive to get closer to it. However, a lifetime of serious and dedicated practice is the only way to move down the road of improvement. I have been made excruciatingly aware of this aspect of kendo, and more so my shortcomings, by training in Japan. It is easy to be the "sensei" back home, but over here, you are just another grunt trying to take another tiny step forward.

The challenge for me now? As I have now returned to my job as a secondary school teacher in New Zealand, how do I engineer my circumstances so that I can somehow do it all again, on some sort of ongoing, and far more regular basis?

MIYAMOTO MUSASHI

A Life in Arms

A BIOGRAPHY OF JAPAN'S GREATEST SWORDSMAN

WILLIAM DE LANGE

INCLUDES THE FIRST ENGLISH TRANSLATION OF THE KOKURA MONUMENT EPITAPH

288 pp, 6 x 9, softcover
11 maps and charts
Lists of historical periods, castles, temples, shrines, battles, and rebellions, glossary, lineages, bibliography, index

Publisher: FLoating World Editions
ISBN: 978-1891640629

FORSAKEN KENDO

Katate guntō-jutsu

By Baptiste Tavernier

Introduction

It is always interesting to see how events connect to form the stream of history. Who would imagine, for example, that one might find a link between an obscure disease called *pébrine*, which plagued France in the second half of the 19th century, and a martial art studied on the other side of the globe in Japan?

Pébrine and *flacherie* are both diseases found in silkworms, and they spread rapidly in Europe from 1855. At that time, France was the world's leading country in sericulture, but the plague of *pébrine* and *flacherie* was going to annihilate, in just a few years, the silkworm population in Lyon and its surrounding area, the country's main centre of silk farming. Many farms and factories went bankrupt, leading to the collapse of the first export industry of Napoleon III's empire: a *catastrophe nationale*!

Most urgent for the farmers was then to find and import a variety of worm that would be immune, or at least resistant, to *pébrine* and *flacherie*. As coincidence would have it, the Japanese silkworm was the most resistant to those diseases, and this very fact precipitated the signature in Edo of the Treaty of Amity and Commerce in October 1858, which marked the official beginning of Franco-Japanese relationships.

By 1864, a large portion of the foreign population in Yokohama was French, and the Ministry of Foreign Affairs thus decided to dispatch Léon Roches to Edo as Plenipotentiary Ambassador, mainly to supervise the trades of worm cocoons and other silk-related affairs. Roches, however, was a very skilful diplomat; he soon became as influential as his British counterpart, Sir Harry Parkes, on the Japanese political scene to the extent that the 14th shogun, Tokugawa Iemochi, declared in a letter addressed to Napoleon III and dated February 15, 1866, his intention to promote Roches to his councillor in foreign affairs (Polack, 2002).

By that time, internal turmoils had shaken Japan and the shogunate was facing uprisings and a possible *coup d'état*: Iemochi's government soon felt the urgency of modernising its military power, both in logistics and theories, and thus addressed an official request to Great Britain and France to envoy qualified military instructors and engineers. The idea was nonetheless welcomed with lukewarm enthusiasm in London, which left the road open for Roches to strengthen a little more the ties between Paris and Edo. Roches, who first came to Japan in order to organise the importation of silkworms, was now playing a prominent role in Japan's military affairs.

The agreement on the first French military mission to Japan was signed by both countries in June 1866. Iemochi's sudden death in August 1866 did not halt the preparations for the mission and finally the French instructors set foot in Yokohama on January 13, 1867.

"French military mission to Japan";
in **Le monde illustré**, *n°503, December 1, 1866.*

The mission was headed by Charles Chanoine, and its purpose was to create a new shogunate army based on a European (more specifically, French) system of both administration/logistics and combat/tactics. Japanese men would receive instruction in artillery, infantry and cavalry.

Unfortunately, the mission fell through shortly after it started. With Tokugawa Yoshinobu's abdication in favour of the Emperor in 1868, the mission was halted and the instructors officially left Japan on October 18, with very little accomplished.

The French military missions and fencing instruction in Japan

With the capture of Napoleon III during the Battle of Sedan (September 1870), and the final defeat in 1871 of the French army in the Franco-Prussian War, one would expect that the newly-formed Meiji government would try to get closer to the German Empire and hire instructors from there in order to continue with the modernisation of Japan's army. However, for several political and economical reasons (silk being one of them) that will not be discussed in this article, Tokyo decided to remain faithful to Paris and agreed for a new military mission as soon as 1872.

The main objectives of the second French military mission to Japan (1872–80) were to establish the Toyama military academy and a national conscription system. There are only scarce sources regarding the teaching of martial techniques by the French instructors at that time. For example, most of the archives kept at the SHD ("Service Historique de la Défense" — the archival records of the French Armed Forces) in Vincennes mainly detail the theoretical courses that students had to attend at the Toyama academy: mathematics, topography, military music, French language, veterinary medicine, etc. Not much is said about artillery or bayonet drills. However, we do know that sergeant François Ducros headed the college of gymnastics from 1874. Military gymnastics, featured callisthenics and also stick handling (*bâton*), which was then regarded as effective introductory training before learning bayonet fencing. Moreover, according to the All Japan Jukendo Federation (Kanesaka, 2007), Ducros, although by no means a specialist in those fields, started to teach fencing and bayonet to his students on a regular basis.

By the time of the third French military mission (1884–89), the shift had finally occurred: Japan now mainly relied on German instruction, and was also hiring advisors from several European countries. Nevertheless, Tokyo decided once again to entrust the land army to

"French officers drilling troops in Osaka in front of the Shogun"; in **L'univers illustré**, n°676, December 28, 1867.

French instruction. The French mission reorganised the Toyama military academy and created in 1886 the four departments of strategy, artillery, callisthenics, and fencing. The fencing course was itself divided into three fields: foil, sabre and bayonet.

We need to pause here, and go back to 1877. During the Satsuma Rebellion, the Battōtai, an elite police squad who fought against Saigo Takamori's forces armed only with swords, rapidly rose in fame. This feat of courage actually led Japan to reconsider its position towards the traditional martial arts that were thought outmoded, and to encourage a revival of *gekken* and *jūjutsu*, especially in the police. The Battōtai was constituted mainly by former *bushi* who would use their *kenjutsu* skills to a devastating effect. The army, on the other hand, had achieved great improvement in artillery but did not have a cohesive close quarter fighting system yet: some soldiers had received instruction in French fencing and bayonet fencing at the Toyama academy, while some had a Japanese *bujutsu* background, but a large number of conscripts simply had no skills at all. The tendency was then to improvise and use imported European weapons like the bayonet or sabre in a "Japanese way", combining, for example, bayonet with *yari* techniques, etc. This state of affairs curiously remained unattended to until the arrival of the third French mission.

The main instructors of the third mission were Etienne de Villaret and Joseph Kiehl. One of their assignments was to create unified fencing and bayonet curricula for the Japanese army, which would be later taught at Toyama's department of fencing. In order to spread this new method, the French advisors would first instruct twelve Japanese noncommissioned officers, who would in turn help teach the techniques to a larger audience. Japanese *kenjutsu* or *sōjutsu* training was strictly forbidden. However, discontent among soldiers was strong. Many

Joseph Kiehl and his students

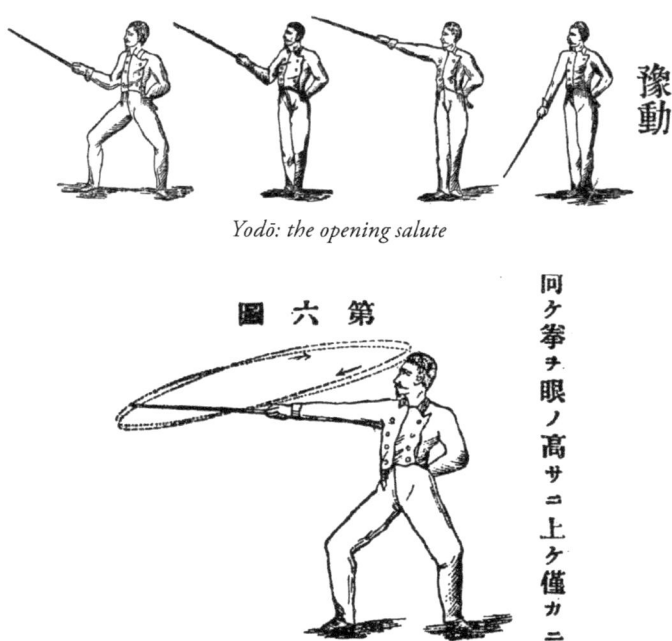

Yodō: the opening salute

Exercise No. 1

in fact favoured *kenjutsu* over sabre, and especially over foil, which they saw as a completely useless system on a real battlefield. Moreover, a rising number of conscripts were becoming skilled in *gekken* and were thus having a hard time becoming accustomed to the European style of fencing, especially to its lunging footwork. Bayonet techniques in France were originally theorised based on traditional fencing, and the ability to lunge was again crucial.

According to Watanabe Ichirō, (1971, p. 899), both Kiehl and de Villaret studied *kenjutsu* from 1887 under Sakakibara Kenkichi. The extent of their study and skills remains, however, unknown. One would wonder if the French officers started *kenjutsu* out of curiosity, or in order to devise a hybrid fencing curriculum that would better suit the Japanese soldiers...

The third French military mission officially ended in January 1889. The same year in November, Japan's Ministry of Army published the *Kenjutsu Kyōhan*, the official fencing textbook that was based on translations of French military teaching materials. The *Kenjutsu Kyōhan* is divided into three volumes:

- Seiken-jutsu (正剣術) —> foil
- Guntō-jutsu (軍刀術) —> sabre
- Jūken-jutsu (銃剣術) —> bayonet

Interestingly enough, Vol. 1 on foil is the longest and most detailed of the three volumes (63 sheets), while the two others on sabre and bayonet are only 22 sheets long. The volume on *guntō-jutsu* is itself divided into three main chapters:

- Definitions and exercises
- Basic drills
- Etiquette and *shiai*

The first chapter, "Definitions and Exercises", starts by explaining the different parts of the sabre, the correct way to grip the hilt and the four moves that constitute the opening salute (*yodō*). The paragraph on footwork and lunges says to refer to the explanations given in Vol. 1 on foil.

In the *Kenjutsu Kyōhan,* fencing concepts such as *fort & faible* (strong part/weak part of the blade), pronation and supination (nails facing downward or upward), or lines (inside-high, outside-low, etc.) are all explained in the foil volume. However, one should note that there is no mention of the parries' names such as *sixte*, *tierce*, *quinte*, *septime*, etc., which would have made the translation easier to read. Instead, the Japanese textbook gives for each technique the position of the blade and the orientation of the nails, in a sometimes confusing way.

The book continues with two exercises that soldiers should perform in order to loosen up their wrist and elbow. The first one consists of stretching the arm out straight forward and whirling the sabre horizontally, and exercise No. 2 asks the practitioner to whirl the sabre vertically.

Those exercises are important because in sabre, strikes are circular (the tip of the blade draws a sort of spiral in the air), so the practitioner needs great mobility in the wrist and elbow.

Before the manual starts detailing strikes and parries, there is one last paragraph, rather unclear, which seems to indicate that *tierce* is preferable to *sixte* as the basic posture in sabre (this would be consistent with modern sabre theory).

After the series of sketches detailing each technique, there is an additional written instruction on *zenhi no zangeki* (slash to the forearm), but it does not feature any illustration:

The edge is facing diagonally downward and the thumb slightly to the right, the position of the right hand should not change much, and while showing the intention of protecting your face (raising the arm), slash the opponent's forearm.

There is no explanation, however, on how to parry that slash to the forearm.

Finally, the chapter ends by detailing the ripostes (counter attacks without lunging—*engeki* in Japanese) that best suits each type of attack.

The second half of the volume on sabre proposes in Chapter 2 numerous examples of drills, and explains how to conduct a training session. Several patterns of attack and riposte are detailed, as well as the commands that officers should shout to the trainees. The last chapter refers to *shiai* rules and etiquette.

Kenjutsu Kyōhan's sabre techniques

Kashira no zangeki / bōfutsu

<u>Slash / parry to the face</u>
Slash: whirl the sabre backward to the left with the edge in front, stretch the arm out and stop the sabre at the height of the opponent's face.
Parry: change the position of the hand in order to have the nails facing forward, raise the arm and keep the edge facing upward. The sabre should be horizontal, slightly in front of the head.

Kata no zangeki / bōfutsu

<u>Slash / parry to the shoulder</u>
Slash: whirl the sabre backward to the left with the edge in front, stretch the arm out and stop the sabre at the height of the opponent's left shoulder.
Parry: Rise and rotate the right arm with the elbow facing outside; the forearm should be horizontal in front of the head [the illustration does not render it clearly], the right wrist is on the centre line, nails facing forward; lower the tip of the sabre with the edge facing left, the blade should be about 10cm apart from the body.

Migi-men no zangeki / bōfutsu

<u>Slash / parry to the right side of the head</u>
Slash: whirl the sabre from right to left with the edge facing to the right, the nails are facing downwards, stretch the arm out and stop the sabre at the height of opponent's head (right side).
Parry: the right hand swerves about 10cm to the right; the edge should be facing right and the blade should slightly lean forward.

Hidari-men no zangeki / bōfutsu

<u>Slash / parry to the left side of the head</u>
Slash: whirl the sabre from left to right with the edge facing to the left, the nails are facing upwards, stretch the arm out and stop the sabre at the height of opponent's head (left side).
Parry: the right hand swerves about 10cm to the left; the edge should be facing left and the blade should slightly lean forward.

Waki no zangeki / bōfutsu

<u>Slash / parry to the side</u>
Slash: the edge is facing diagonally upward and the thumb slightly to the left, stretch the arm out and stop the sabre at the opponent's right side.
Parry: the right hand swerves outward to the right, with the elbow facing outside; the forearm should be horizontally aligned with the shoulder; lower the tip of the sabre with the edge facing right, the blade should be about 33cm away from the body

Hara no zangeki / bōfutsu

<u>Slash / parry to the abdomen</u>
Slash: the edge is facing diagonally upward and the thumb slightly to the right, stretch the arm out and stop the sabre at the level of the opponent's abdomen.
Parry: rise and rotate the right arm with the elbow facing out; the forearm should be horizontally aligned with the shoulder, the right wrist is on the centreline, nails facing forward; lower the tip of the sabre with the edge facing left, the blade should be about 10cm away from the body.

Totsugeki / bōfutsu

<u>Thrust / parry</u>
Thrust: lower the tip of the sabre at the level of the chest, rotate the wrist so the thumb faces downward and the edge upward, stretch the arm out and lunge.
Parry: lower slightly the tip of the sabre, while the right hand swerves towards the centre of the body.

From French sabre to Japanese *katate guntō-jutsu*

One may wonder why the Ministry of Army decided to promote a *Kenjutsu Kyōhan* based on the contested French military fencing. After all, the book was published almost one year after the official end of the French mission, so Tokyo had the opportunity to abandon that system and come back instead to *gekken*/kendo, since many officers and soldiers were already skilled in Japanese *kenjutsu*.

In fact, it seems first that a faction at the Toyama academy was still strongly in favour of the French method. Secondly, the army was facing an unforeseen problem: Japan had already adopted (and ordered) the European sabre as its standard weapon, and it certainly seemed far too costly to re-equip officers and soldiers with *katana* instead. Nevertheless, one year after the publication of the *Kenjutsu Kyōhan*, Baron Ōkubo Haruno, then-director of the Toyama academy declared that French fencing was not suited to Japanese people's morphology and spirit, and recommended *gekken* instead. He thus asked Tsuda Kyōjū (the reading of the given name is uncertain), chief of the gymnastic department and successor of the Tsuda Ichiden-ryū, to devise a new system (Kanesaka, 2007). Tsuda's research led to the publication of a revised version of the *Kenjutsu Kyōhan* in April 1894.

The first main difference with the 1889 edition of the

book is its division into only two sections, *guntō-jutsu* and *jūken-jutsu*: *seiken-jutsu*, the foil, has been completely removed from the official guidelines. The next striking difference is in the training equipment: the new system advocates the use of *shinai* and *bōgu*, and is thus in this respect very close to Japanese *gekken*.

However, a closer look at the guidelines reveals that in fact, the technical syllabus of the 1894's *guntō-jutsu* (this is also the case for *jūken-jutsu*) is still largely based on the 1889's French one. First of all, the techniques described here form indeed a one-handed (*katate*) sword system, as opposed to the traditional two-handed (*morote*) Japanese *kenjutsu*. The hilt of a European sabre does not easily allow handling the weapon with two hands, and since the whole army was equipped with such a sword, Tsuda had to cope with it.

The footwork has been changed to better suit the Japanese soldiers and thus the deep lunge has been abolished in favour of leaping strikes. Nonetheless, a shallow lunge is still performed at the end of the attack (this is still the case in modern jukendo and tankendo). Finally, the strikes themselves are still performed in the sabre (circular) fashion with the tip of the *shinai* drawing a spiral before hitting. The structure of the revised *Kenjutsu Kyōhan* follows also the structure of the old version, with the same points discussed in the same order, often with the same vocabulary.

Some technical elements of European fencing have however been expurgated. The lunge, as mentioned above, is now very shallow. Neither the concept of pronation/supination or the fencing lines are explained anymore. *Yodō* has also been abandoned, replaced by a more Japanese style of *reigi*.

1894's *guntō-jutsu* is therefore a hybrid system that mixes European sabre and Japanese *gekken*. Basic techniques are explained in short paragraphs, which feature an illustration.

2nd edition's *guntō-jutsu* techniques

Men (sayū-men) no zangeki

<u>Slash to the head (and both sides of the head)</u>
Whirl your sabre backward and immediately slash the face (or the side of the head) of your opponent.

Zenhi (kote) no zangeki

<u>Slash to the forearm</u>
Whirl the sabre backward to the left and immediately slash the opponent's right forearm.

Totsugeki (tsuki)

<u>Thrust</u>
Stretch your arm out, (the wrist can rotate either left or right), while stepping forward and thrust to the throat.
[**Note:** In these guidelines, a *tsuki* to the *mengane* is deemed valid, whereas a thrust to the chest or the abdomen is not.]

Migi-dō no zangeki

<u>Slash to the right side</u>
Whirl the sabre to the left and immediately slash the opponent's right side.

Hidari-dō no zangeki

Slash to the left side
Whirl the sabre to the right and immediately slash the opponent's left side.

Men (sayū-men) no bōfutsu

 or

Block to the head (and both sides of the head)
Stretch out the arm and raise the wrist (the wrist should rotate left or right in order to block strikes coming from the side) to the level of your eyes; the tip of the blade should be slightly diagonal towards the opponent. A block can be performed close to your head, or far away in the direction of the opponent.
[**note:** the guidelines stipulate that all blocks should be performed with the edge of the sword, never with the back nor the sides, as those parts are considered weak.]

Totsugeki no bōfutsu

Blocking tsuki
When blocking a thrust (left or right), do it forward in direction of the opponent.

Zenhi no bōfutsu

Block to the forearm
When blocking the slash coming from the outside (inside), stretch your arm out [towards the opponent] slightly to the right (left).

Hidari-dō, migi-dō no bōfutsu

Block to the left or right side
When blocking the slash to the side (right or left), swerve your arm downward to the right (left) while keeping the tip of the sword diagonally upward.

The decline of *katate guntō-jutsu*

After the end of the Russo-Japanese War (1905), voices raised in the Japanese army judged that the *guntō-jutsu* was not effective enough, and that it should be researched thoroughly and perfected.

A new revision of the *Kenjutsu Kyōhan* was thus published in 1907, in which circular strikes are now abandoned in favour of kendo *furiage* strikes. From that edition onward, strikes to the forearm would become gradually disregarded.

A new category of *guntō-jutsu* appears in the 1907 textbook: *jōba guntō-jutsu* or *guntō-jutsu* on horseback.

However from 1915, the Japanese army decided to discard the sabre system and to promote instead the two-handed *morote guntō-jutsu*, a modified version of kendo for military use (outdoor training only, no dojo footwork and no left *dō* strikes—at that time, the soldier's equipment effectively protected the left side of the torso). The old *guntō-jutsu* would be then renamed *katate guntō-jutsu*, as opposed to *morote guntō-jutsu* and practised only by cavalry officers.

From 1919, the Japanese army devised a new one-handed close-quarter combat system called *tanken-jutsu*, based on detached bayonet fighting and Japanese *kodachi* techniques. As a result, *katate guntō-jutsu* slowly disappeared as bayonet and detached bayonet techniques become the main curricula before and during World War II.

When the ban on budo was lifted by the GHQ a few years after the war, only *jūken-jutsu* and *tanken-jutsu* were revived as "Japanese martial ways", and transformed into jukendo and tankendo. *Katate guntō-jutsu* was completely forsaken and did not evolve into a modern budo.

Jōba guntō-jutsu

References.
- Archives du Service Historique de la Défense, Vincennes
- Kanesaka Hiromichi (editor), *Jūkendō Hyaku-nen Shi*, Tokyo, Zen Nihon Jūkendō Renmei Jimukyoku, 2007
- *Kenjutsu Kyōhan*, Kobayashi Matashichi, 1889
- *Kenjutsu Kyōhan*, Kobayashi Matashichi, 1894
- *Kenjutsu Kyōhan*, Kōseidō, 1907
- *Kenjutsu Kyōhan*, Gun'yū Kyōkai, 1915
- Polak Christian, *Sabre et Pinceau*, Tokyo, CCIFJ, 2005
- Polak Christian, *Soie et Lumières*, Tokyo, Hachette Fujingaho, 2002
- Watanabe Ichirō, *Meiji Budō Shi*, Tokyo, Shinjinbutsu Hōraisha 1971

Musō Jikiden Eishin-ryū Riai
The Meaning of the Kata: Part 1

By Kim Taylor

Introduction

This series of articles is an explanation of the meaning behind the *kata* of the Musō Jikiden Eishin-ryū (MJER) and the organization of those *kata* into their levels and order. I claim no special knowledge of the thoughts of Ōe Masamichi as I was not alive when he reorganised the school into its present order. I simply offer my thoughts on this from a background of 30 years practice in the school and in some other Japanese sword arts. Please understand while you are reading this that it is one person's way of organising and understanding the material. You are encouraged to read this, compare it with what you have been taught and what you understand, and come to your own conclusions.

Background

In the early 1600s, Hayashizaki Jinsuke Minamoto Shigenobu (c1546-c1621) developed the Shinmei Musoryū, also known as the Shin Musō Hayashizaki-ryū, the art that would eventually become the Musō Jikiden Eishin-ryū. "Musō" means "matchless" or "peerless", and "*jikiden*" means "directly transmitted".

Hasegawa Chikaranosuke Eishin (Hidenobu) learned the style in Edo between 1716 and 1735. Recognised as the 7th headmaster of this lineage he had a great influence on the art. From him the line then went to Hayashi Rokudayu Morimasa (1661-1732), the 9th headmaster, who took the art from Edo (present-day Tokyo) to the Tosa domain in Shikoku where it remained until the late 19th century.

A swordsman by the name of Ōmori Rokurōzaemon Masamitsu practised the style under Eishin in Edo. He was also a student of Ogasawara-ryū Reihō and was said to have developed a set of *iai kata* from the *seiza* posture, which he then taught to Hayashi Rokudayu.

The school remained in Tosa for many generations, taught in two lines—the Tanimura and the Shimomura—and eventually came down to Ōe Masamichi Shikei (1852-1927) who studied both lines but became the 17th headmaster of the Tanimura-ha. During the tenure of Ōe, Nakayama Hakudō, a famous swordsman from Tokyo, came to Tosa to learn *iai*. He took it back to Tokyo and his practice eventually became known as the Musō Shinden-ryū.

Ōe Masamichi and Standardizaion

At the time of Ōe Masamichi, the school would seem to have been a loose accumulation of *kata* from various eras. Between 1912-1926, Ōe standardised the *kata* from both Eishin and Ōmori into the current three levels, and established it as the Musō Jikiden Eishin-ryū. In my part of the world the levels are called "Ōmori-ryū", "Eishin-ryū", and "Oku Iai Iwaza" and "Oku Iai Tachi Waza". We commonly accept that the Oku Iai are the oldest techniques, handed down from Hayashizaki, and that the Eishin-ryū and Ōmori techniques are from Eishin and Ōmori respectively. Other names for the levels also exist: Ōmori-ryū is called "Shōden"; Eishin-ryū, "Chūden"; and the Oku Iai are sometimes known as "Hayashizaki-ryū". When talking about the Musō Shinden-ryū, the terms "Shoden", "Chūden" and "Oku Iai" are used by our local students, and they also use an alternate set of names for the Shōden level, although the *kata* remain broadly the same.

This will be discussed further as the articles progress, but it should be understood that over 17 generations of a martial art, the attributing of various *kata* to specific headmasters could be more a matter of convenience and convention than historical fact. Training in budo is concerned with present physical practice first, and historical records only incidentally. Put more bluntly, knowing the hagiography of the school is little help in the physical practice of the art itself.

Of Swords and Tatami

In order to perform iaido as we know it, we must be using a katana, a sword placed in the belt with the edge up. The first curved, single-edged long swords in Japan were mounted *tachi* style, with the edge down and carried by hangers dropping from the obi. From the mid-1400s, a new style of wearing the sword through the belt with the edge up was created by dismounted lower ranked warriors which was called "*uchi-gatana*". By 1600 it had come to be named "katana" and was the dominant way to wear a long sword for all ranks. We can see that Hayashizaki would likely have created his sword drawing art with the most common style of sword in mind, hence there is probably no need to speculate that iaido was originally performed with *tachi* and later with katana.

Having said that, it is necessary to draw the *tachi* using the left and right hands in pretty much the same way as we do in our standard iaido practice. In fact, while we can draw the smaller sword through the belt with a single hand, using the pressure of the stomach on the *saya* to keep it fixed in the obi, this would be much more difficult with the *tachi*. Any *kata* from the MJER could as easily be performed with the *tachi* as with the katana. Using the *tachi* mount would in fact allow the use of much longer swords as the katana's *saya* can only be moved so far back into the *obi*, while a *tachi saya* could be moved behind the hip during the draw.

MJER is performed from standing, *tate-hiza* (one knee standing) and *seiza*. It is usually presumed that the *seiza* style of sitting originated with the practice of using tatami in the house. Tatami rooms appeared in the houses of the upper classes during the Muromachi period (1337-1573) and *seiza* became a formal way to sit. By 1700 most Japanese used *seiza* as their formal sitting position, but before this—in Hayashizaki's time—the formal sitting method seems to have been *tate-hiza*, to sit on one knee with the other foot flat on the ground and the knee straight up.

Assuming the school was developed for practical purposes during a period of war and unrest, we can speculate that Hayashizaki developed techniques from the most common positions; from standing as well as *tate-hiza*. By the time of Eishin, Ōmori and Hayashi, the most common sitting position was *seiza* so it would make sense to create a set of techniques using this as the starting position. Hence, the standing and *tate-hiza* techniques of Oku Iai could be thought of as the oldest techniques, the *tate-hiza* techniques of Eishin as derivatives of those, and the *seiza* techniques of Ōmori-ryū as derivatives of the earlier *kata* performed from the new sitting position.

Assumptions

First, we will assume that *kata* are best described as an *aide memoire* rather than a patterned response. In other words, the *kata* exist to teach us the *kihon* and to give us ways in which to practise them. The *kihon* are the fundamental ideas of the school itself, being the cuts, deflections, thrusts and evasions that one puts together during an encounter. The *kata* are often said to be patterned responses to attacks which are somehow, one has to assume, predictable in advance. I am convinced this is not so. I am also convinced that these are not actions "discovered on the battlefield".

Second, in order to analyse the school, it is necessary to assume that one does not practise the All Japan Kendo Federation *iai* (Seitei-gata) or similar composite sets of *kata* from other organizations. These composite sets are an abbreviation of the schools and usually include techniques from two or more levels of practice. They are certainly not, as some people assume, a "basic set" of techniques that one does before learning a *koryū*. The MJER had its own basic set (Ōmori-ryū) and advanced practice (Eishin and Oku) and we must examine them as they are, not from the viewpoint of experience in any other art.

With the above background and history of MJER, we should now examine why Ōe Masamichi set the school into its current organisation. We learn the sets in the order of Ōmori, Eishin and then Oku Iai. Why did Ōe decide on this order, and why did he position the order of the *kata* within the sets as he did? What and how do we learn as we go along through the *kata*?

Beginning Set: The Ōmori-ryū

Here is where a beginner to iaido starts, with this set of 11 techniques, mostly from *seiza*. It is the youngest of the three levels of practice, adopted by the 9th headmaster, Hayashi Rokudayu sometime in the early 1700s. If most Japanese sat formally in *seiza* by this time it would be easiest for students to start learning from this position. While this is sufficient reason in itself, *seiza* also has various other advantages as a beginning: it cuts out any use of the ankles and knees, making more stable postures for drawing and cutting. The hips will start and stay square out of *seiza* by default rather than by effort. If both *seiza* and *tate-hiza* are new ways of sitting for the student, it will be easier to start forward and move out of *seiza* compared to *tate-hiza* as it is easier to teach the application of forward power.

The basic characteristic of the Ōmori-ryū is a horizontal cut from the scabbard followed by a vertical cut. The horizontal cut is in fact a characteristic of the entire MJER, and it is easiest to perform with the cross draw that results from the *saya* at the left hip and drawing with the right hand. A horizontal cut allows you to expand your chest which allows the hip to transfer power into the tip of the sword. If you are in an MJER line that performs *saya-biki* (there are those who do not), that movement is easiest (largest) when done in a horizontal move around the hip. A horizontal cut is the most powerful arc of the blade from the *saya*; any other arc involves a complicated shoulder movement which will weaken the connection between hip and tip. Finally, a horizontal cut must be done cleanly and smoothly as the kneeling position combines with the motion to eliminate any falling weight or rising muscle in the cut. This means the power must come entirely from good technique.

The vertical finishing cut is done two-handed so this movement is best/easiest to perform in a balanced way from a square-to-the-front hip position with the hands dropping from overhead. By learning to close the armpits it is easy to powerfully drop the hips into the cut adding the body weight to the technique to create a powerful strike. Angled cuts from overhead are also possible, but the school has chosen the vertical cut.

Nuki-tsuke

Mae (Shohatto)

There are four basic parts to most *iai kata* and they are *nuki-tsuke*, the draw and cut from the scabbard; *kiri-tsuke*, the finishing cut or cuts; *chiburi* (or *chiburui*), cleaning the blade; and *nōtō*, the replacement of the blade into the scabbard. Mae is a good representation of this set of movements.

Nuki-tsuke

This is basic. A horizontal cut across the opponent's shoulders as he rises and attacks means this is a *sen-no-sen* (attack into the attack) technique. Philosophically, this is the easiest type of situation to understand as a beginner: The opponent has attacked first but you "beat him to the punch". The situation is simple; you are clearly allowed to counterattack if attacked, so there is no moral ambiguity.

The draw is done by pressing the *tsukagashira* toward the opponent and releasing the tip at *saya-banare* so that the right (drawing) hand closes to apply the *kissaki* to the target. The chest is then expanded, the lower shoulder blades contracted with the *saya-biki* movement, and the cut made. The movement forward should be done in a single drive so that the hips rise as the thighs pivot at the knees. The toes will be flipped under as the legs move into position. Both feet should be planted as contact is made with the target or the energy of the cut will be lost. Beginners may be told to rise, flip the toes under and then cut but this should be a transition technique until they can feel the difference between up and forward, and just forward, up being a consequence of one's leg construction.

Saya-biki

As noted above, some lines do not practise *saya-biki*, the movement of the scabbard back away from the tip at *saya-banare*. This is because the swords we use now tend to be longer than the ones originally used in MJER. Drawing a longer sword is easier if the *saya* is moved with the blade. This change is a simple demonstration of how the school will respond to external factors, such as the desire to use longer blades. Again, techniques are not set in stone; they change according to the situation.

Kiri-tsuke

The sword is returned so that first the tip, then the *monouchi* and finally the *tsukagashira* is aiming at the opponent as the blade moves overhead and a vertical cut is made downward through the opponent's head so that the tip ends up slightly downward to exit the groin. This of course assumes the opponent is up on his knees; if he is not, this tip-down position will still ensure the blade exits the body.

Note that in some lines the kneeling cuts are finished

Kiri-tsuke

Chiburi

in a horizontal position rather than tip-down. Does this mean that those lines finish with the tip in the body? Of course not. Our lineage states that we finish tip-down to exit the body, but this is simply an explanation for beginners. As was mentioned earlier, *kata* are stories that allow us to practise the *kihon*, so they are not, in that respect, "real". If you cut deeply into the body in front of you, your blade will still be inside the body when you finish with the tip downward. If you cut shallowly, cutting only the face, your tip will finish outside the opponent even if you finish at throat height.

Chiburi

The *chiburi* movement is done not so much to shake blood off of the blade, as is usually stated, but in order to stand, bring the two feet together and look at the opponent in a movement of *zanshin*. The technique is not over at this point, so *chiburi* is done by controlling the opponent with *kissaki*, *monouchi* and *tsukagashira* on the way upward, and then *monouchi* and *kissaki* on the way down to "shake off the blood". Again, this movement of *chiburi* and checking the opponent is not difficult for a beginner to understand, so it is explained in this way. The usual MJER *chiburi* is done with the tip remaining below the *tsuka* so that the blood does not drain into the hilt, which would cause problems. This consideration may prevent the *tsukagashira* from being aimed at the opponent while the hilt is held near the forehead, but the edge can still be angled in such a way as to be a threat.

We say this movement is a shaking off of the blood, but it could also be considered as simply representative of cleaning the blade (blood is sticky and is better wiped off

Nōtō

無雙直傳英信流居合術

than shaken). It can also simply be thought of as a way to put the blade into a position to make the next movement.

Old Man Iai and Chiburi

The position of the body at *chiburi* is often cited as an example where students could show "old man's iai". By throwing the head forward and bending at the waist during the first part of this move it is easier to stand up from the kneeling position, and it is presumed that old men do this. In fact, one reason for putting the feet together is so that one can peer at the opponent to see if he is still a threat, and leaning forward can be seen as part of this process. Yet young men can stand up with good posture (straight backs) using their strong legs and still look down (with their not near-sighted eyes) and check the opponent without leaning over. This is now considered a more powerful and beautiful movement and there is no particular harm doing it this way, as long as the meaning of the movement is understood.

Nōtō

If we are to do another *kata* we must put the blade back into the scabbard at some point, so it is no surprise that we do it now. Since we are putting the blade away before moving back we should keep demonstrating *zanshin*, maintain a sense of style and position, control the fallen opponent with the movement of the sword, feel that we are gathering in power to use in case we need to respond to a further attack, and many other things as well. But mostly we are getting ready to perform the next *kata*.

Satō

無雙直傳英

Enbu, Merihari and Kihon

The important part of any *kata* is the *kihon*, the basic movements of the school. A *kata* happens when we string *kihon* together to practise responses to attacks, so make a story, give a bit of an *enbu*, a performance. The iaido student should show by using *merihari*—the balance between tension and relaxation, fast and slow movements—what is happening during the *kata*. *Iai* is a way to practise solo, using a real blade. The practice should be as realistic as we can make it. There is no actual feedback from a competitor or an opponent, so we must use creative visualisation to test our skill. The story of the *kata* should be clear.

Migi (Satō)

This is Mae to the left and not much deeper in meaning than that. We turn to the right and sit so that our opponent is coming from our left. The command "*migi*" means to turn to the right. The Musō Shinden-ryū use the term "*satō*", which means "the sword from the left". These names cause endless amusement.

The turn to the left gives the student practice in turning and cutting while in *seiza*, and the ideal way is to do this with as few moves and as little fuss as possible.

Move the right knee to the left or you will move back from the opponent as you raise your hips (move forward from your seated position). Your weight will naturally move onto the right knee, allowing you to lift your left

信流居合術

Utō

knee and spiral upward while you draw. The right toes move down and under as the turn is finished; the left toes simply move under as the foot is rolled to the left. This motion may be difficult for beginners so they can be told to rise straight up, flip the toes under and then turn, but eventually the smoother spiral movement should be done.

The left foot can be moved into its final *nuki-tsuke* position as you turn or it can be rolled into position and then driven forward as you cut horizontally making this movement the same as the thrust forward in Mae. The right hand moves directly toward the opponent as the turn is made, picking up the *tsuka* on the way and drawing directly at the opponent's *suigetsu*. There should be no feeling of drawing out and around, as this leaves the swordsman exposed to a counterattack. The rest of the *kata* should be identical to Mae, with the legs reversed.

Hidari (Utō)

This is Mae to the right and all the points about turning in Migi also apply to Hidari. The student now knows how to turn in both directions, and the hips are balanced so that both hips can now be felt when doing Mae. The left hand moves across the body and delivers the *tsuka* into the right hand on this technique so that the draw is again made directly at the opponent.

Part 2 of this series will continue with the remaining *kata* of the Ōmori-ryū: Ushiro, Yae-gaki, Uke-nagashi, Kaishaku, Tsuke-komi, Tsuki-kage, Oi-kaze and Nuki-uchi.

The Great *Hagakure* Paradox
—An Affirmation of Life?

Alexander Bennett Ph.D.

Properly titled *Hagakure-kikigaki* (literally "Dictations given hidden by leaves"), *Hagakure* is undeniably the most infamous treatise on *bushido*, and possibly the most misunderstood. Completed in 1716, it consists of 11 books containing approximately 1,300 aphorisms and contemplations concerning the people, history, and culture of the Saga domain in the southern Japanese island of Kyushu. The first two books of *Hagakure* were dictated by Yamamoto Jōchō (Tsunetomo 1659–1719), a middle-ranking retainer of Lord Nabeshima Mitsushige (1632–1700), to fellow clansman Tashiro Tsuramoto (1678–1748). Books 3 to 6 are about the Nabeshima lords and episodes that occurred in the Saga domain; Books 7 to 9 delve into the "meritorious feats" of Saga warriors; Book 10 is a critique of samurai from other provinces; and Book 11 provides supplementary information about miscellaneous events and various aspects of warrior culture.

Some of the vignettes are short and to the point; but others are quite long and convoluted, and difficult to make sense of without a sound contextual understanding of the dilemmas faced by samurai in a time of peace. In a nutshell, *Hagakure* is a memoir of Jōchō's service in the Nabeshima clan chronicling the feats of individual samurai, and the trials and tribulations of trying to succeed in the samurai's community of honour. It serves as a fascinating window into the maelstrom of retainership and the strong emotional bonds that bound vassal and lord. It is violent in places, slightly erotic in others, but seeks to clarify the purest kind of "hidden love" represented by absolute and selfless devotion to one's overlord. Jōchō was so enamoured with his lord that his greatest desire was to martyr himself and follow him to the afterlife. To his chagrin, the practice of self-immolation known as *junshi* had already been outlawed, so he retired from the mundane world and took the tonsure instead. It was at whose hermitage shaded by the trees that Tsuramoto interviewed Jōchō in his twilight years.

Some of the stories are told with thoughtful reflection, and others are passionate rants about the ideal mindset for a warrior. Rather than being a well-ordered philosophical discourse on *bushido*, the content represents an emotional rollercoaster ride, randomly plunging the reader into the darkest chasms of insanity, only to bring the tone back to a profound sense of equanimity and acceptance of the ephemeral nature of our existence. There is even the odd smattering of humour to be gleaned from the pages if one looks for it.

Hagakure's underlying theme of absolute loyalty to one's lord to the extent that a warrior must be "prepared to die" in the course of duty—a notion symbolised by the legendary phrase, "The Way of the warrior is to be found in dying" (*Bushidō to iu wa shinu koto to mitsuketari*). The anonymous hero of the discourse is the *kusemono*—that being a warrior who remains inconspicuous when things are calm in the realm, but can be relied on in times of calamity to serve his lord with matchless effectiveness and vigour, with no concern for self-preservation.

In fact, Jōchō asserts that the only way a warrior can reach the praiseworthy heights of exemplary service is to live as if he was already dead—to know that each and every moment could be his last. As long as he was prepared for his imminent death, then he would be liberated from the shackles of egotistic desire, and his life would be so much more meaningful for it. Different ranks of samurai had distinctive duties and responsibilities, but self-sacrifice (death) predicated on fanatical service to lord and clan was emblematic of personal honour, and was ultimately the defining moment of an admirable life.

Predictably, such notions of total self-sacrifice fitted well with the designs of Japan's militaristic machine before and during WWII. Most readers will immediately conjure up images of kamikaze pilots and their one-way missions to certain death. Indeed, pilots were not unknown to have pocket-sized editions of *Hagakure* in their jackets as they zoomed to their doom. That is why the book was shunned in the post-war period as representing an irrational and repugnant ideal that glorified meaningless death and warmongering. Books such as *Hagakure* were subjected to intense criticism as being tools for militaristic propaganda that sought to instil Japanese youth with an indomitable sense of patriotism, and prepare them to discard their own lives for the emperor and the mother country. *Hagakure* provided a powerful and emotive creed for wartime ultranationalists, in no small part due to its one-dimensional affirmation of loyalty to the point of "frenzied death" (*shini-gurui*). Was this, however, a fair interpretation of what Jōchō really meant?

Hagakure provides the reader with a window into the confusing predicament of samurai, professional warriors, in Pax-Tokugawa (1603-1868). Although Jōchō often comes across as a disgruntled old curmudgeon, grumpy at the degeneration of the age, one can detect method in his madness by reading between the lines.

After painstakingly translating *Hagakure* over the last four years, I came to the realisation that Jōchō's morbid infatuation with death was actually an affirmation of life. It is possible to take his words literally, as the militarists did. In the course of translating the text, however, I was especially careful to avoid judging the content from a contemporary moral stance (as much as that is possible). I also tried not to conveniently fashion his words into something that would have more significance to modern readers. Instead, I tried to 'communicate' with Jōchō (and Tsuramoto for that matter), and get to the crux of his angst and intent, contextualised by an historical understanding of samurai society. Although this also has its limitations, I feel that I was able to tap into the spirit that underlies Jōchō's sentiments.

Is *Hagakure* a useful book for understanding samurai military strategy? To a certain extent, but unlike other classic samurai treatises like Miyamoto Musashi's *Gorin-no-Sho*, it is not a book on strategy per se. Will it help your study of the martial arts? Certainly not from a technical perspective. Will it assist you in your comprehension of the didactic culture of the samurai, and the essence of that nebulous term '*bushido*'? Absolutely! And by virtue of that, it will certainly provide the reader with valuable clues for accessing the fundamental philosophy of Japanese martial arts. It is a stretch to claim that the "wisdom of the samurai" extracted from the pages of *Hagakure* will be life changing. Nevertheless, read with an open mind, *Hagakure* will press the reader to confront the reality of his or her mortality—the transience of all things.

On the surface, *Hagakure* is fraught with contradiction. A careful study of the text, however, will reveal that the seemingly paradoxical lessons being spiritedly espoused by Jōchō are in fact interdependent pieces of the puzzle of life. The biggest such paradox is the view that embracing the inevitability of one's death (both figuratively and literally) is the most productive and honourable way to live.

Shinai Sagas
Always Armed

By Charlie Kondek

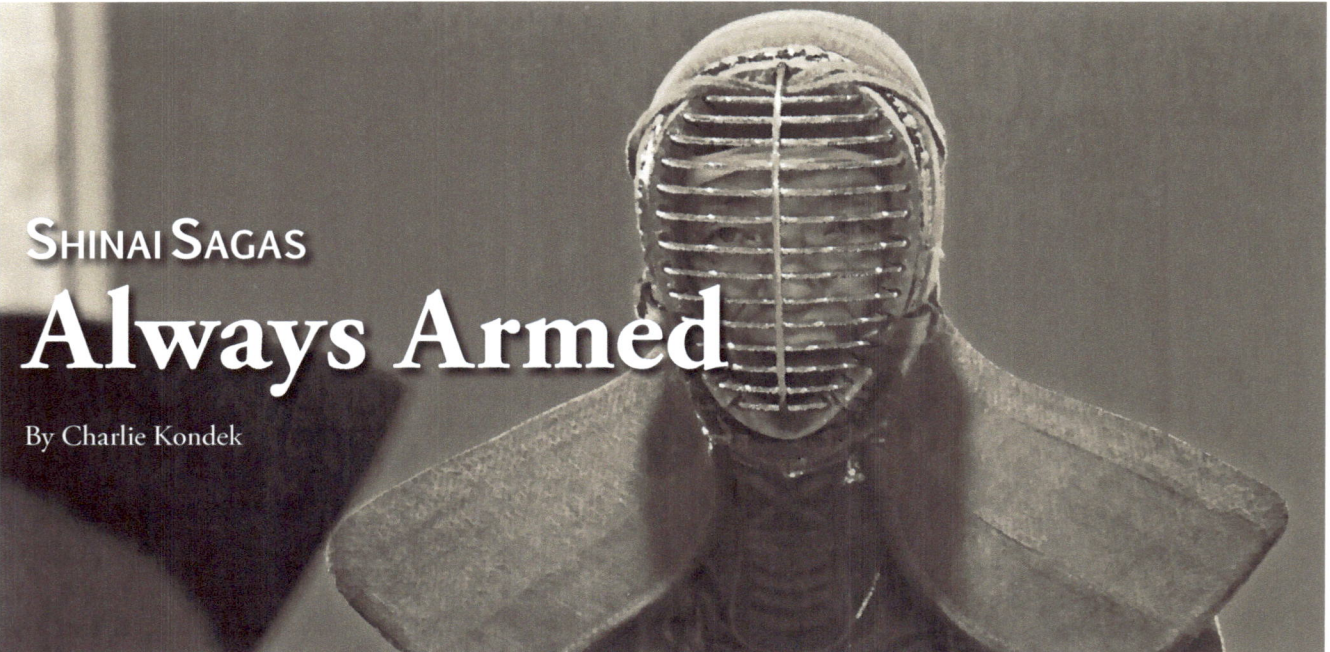

He was at a party with some friends, and he found himself talking with a karate black belt about the similarities between karate and kendo. Two more guys joined the conversation, and as the talk began to include them, he realized he knew one of the newcomers by reputation—an obnoxious man, especially when drinking, which they all were.

This man, apparently acutely sensitive to how he was perceived by his friend, perhaps also hoping to impress some of the girls that might overhear, began to irritate the martial arts students with rude remarks. "You guys think you're a couple bad asses, huh?" He leaned back on his heels and gestured with his beer, held at the level of his belt. "Man, I got a shotgun at home that would tear both of you to pieces—*sha-shik*!" He mimed pumping a shell into the weapon. "Where's all that karate gonna get you when you're staring down the barrel of a gun? Huh?" He was clearly performing, but now he began to seem genuinely offended, as if Mazurski and the karate student had provoked him and not the other way around, as if what had started as a joke at someone else's expense became a realisation. Who the hell did they think they were?

*

He and his boss emerged gratefully from the buzz of the crowded lobby at the centre of the enormous glass building, shedding the weight of the previous four hours as they made their way to the waiting cab. They hadn't talked much in the elevator.

"I think that went well."

"Well, as well as could be expected, but I think we're gonna be okay."

Now, as the car made its way through the corporate park to the freeway, they debriefed.

"Yeah, that went well. We were very well prepared. God, these people."

From there to the airport they inventoried the personalities in the room and the role each had played in contributing to the present situation, a massive *mea culpa* in which they had carefully chronicled, with documentation Mazurski had extensively, obsessively assembled and ordered, that which could reasonably be laid at the feet of the vendor, that which could be attributed to the client, and the various states of confusion and misery that had arisen as a result of the actions between the two. All of this carefully sheltered in language meant to prevent any alienation —words like "lessons learned" and "pivot away", "enfranchise stakeholders", "cascade solutions" —and encourage them to move forward with a working relationship until the current projects were completed. Mazurski, the budding young account executive, had set up points for his boss, the old campaigner, to volley back and forth with the clients, toggling as they went between project plans and appendices, email chains and scope revisions, for projects that were late and over budget, missing components or functioning below benchmarks, which the clients in their bickering and ineptitude had undermined and which a larger, more experienced firm might have handled better.

On the airport concourse, Mazurski's boss led him to a bar near their gate.

"Don't even open your laptop," he said. "What are you drinking?"

With the first sip of the double bourbon, layers of tension slid from his shoulders. Mazurski opened a button on his shirt and gratefully sank another inch into the barstool.

Mazurski's boss, 15 years older and with thinning, wiry hair and fleshy red cheeks, himself relaxed into a vodka and cranberry and said behind the ice at the bottom of the glass, "You did good work on this, Mike. You got us all the way here. I tell you, account work isn't for everyone but I think you have a good grasp of it. Plenty of this crap is our fault but just as much if not more is theirs. It's like we always say, accounts stand between clients and development and your arms aren't long enough to reach both. You gotta move 'em both toward the middle and it's like moving glaciers sometimes." He signalled for a second drink. "But you're doing a good job. Everybody likes you. Where'd you learn to be like that?"

An explanation leaped to Mazurski's lips but he held it behind his teeth, chose different words. What his boss said was true, he felt. How could he say without context, without inviting confusion and more explanation that would have wearied the conversation, where he got his instincts for this kind of work?

He put it this way: "Well, I try to read the situation and identify who is owed what or what the obligations are. You know? I'm kind of constantly paying attention to the people in the mix and trying to anticipate who gets what and how that's articulated. I assume everyone has good intentions but is working within the confines of their own point of view or their own limits, and I facilitate the right response to each." He shrugged and, before the glass reached his lips, added, "And, you know, I say 'please' and 'thank you' and 'sorry.'" His boss laughed.

He wanted to add that kendo had made in him an instinct for *rei* and he had discerned there were *reigi* for everything, particularly the workplace. But he couldn't think of a way to add that in a way that was appropriate to a conversation with his boss in an airport bar. How could he say it without sounding heavy, or preachy, or weird?

*

Perspiration cooling on his brow, he knelt beside where Skenazy sat in *seiza* tugging at his *dō-himo*. He took *seiza* himself and said, "How was practice? Good? Drink?"

"Practice, yes, I needed that," Skenazy said. "And a drink, I could use that, too."

"Rough day?"

"I'm breaking up with Marjorie. I just decided."

The ordeal had tormented Paul Skenazy for a year. Somehow since moving in with her, his enthusiasm and Marjorie's had diverged, or, rather, Marjorie had lost interest and let things slip into an indifference that they struggled to escape. They reconstructed that dreadful year at the restaurant afterward. Most of Skenazy's friends insisted she was taking advantage of him. The problem was he still loved her. She said she loved him, too.

"But I can't keep living like this."

"Can't, or won't?"

"Can't, won't, it doesn't matter."

On the sidewalk outside with a few beers in him, Skenazy was more candid with Mazurski and Nygaard.

"I don't want to do this. She doesn't want to do this. It feels like I'm severing a limb. I'm going to be full of regret. But it's done. I've decided."

These last two words with a simple exhalation that settled his shoulders under his jacket, his hands in his pockets. "If it's one thing I've learned from kendo, it's how to be decisive. Make your decision and take what comes."

"Have you told her yet? Don't tell her tonight," suggested Nygaard.

"Tomorrow morning," said Skenazy. "Over coffee. That's a good time to have a conversation like that."

They offered to walk with him but he preferred to go alone, and the last they saw was his slight stumble into the night beneath the *shinai* and *bōgu* bags slung over his shoulder.

Shinai Sagas

There were only a few weeks left on the lease and Skenazy found another place in the meantime, but the opportunity to move out came up quickly. Mazurski got an apologetic, urgent text asking for help. He dropped what he was doing and showed up at Skenazy's place with his car. "Marjorie here?" Mazurski asked when Skenazy came to the door. "At work," was the reply. Mazurski was relieved. Half of Skenazy's apartment was in boxes and plastic laundry baskets or stuffed into paper bags. "Thank you so much for coming," Skenazy said. "I texted a bunch of people but I'm not sure who's going to make it on such short notice."

"Let's see what we can cram in my car." They laboured up and down the steps. It was one of the last warm days, the end of summer in a college town. All around them as they carried boxes and bags were the lazy motions of people for whom there were no drastic changes. Marjorie's absence from the scene was welcome but the lingering air of her presence was known in the hallway and beneath the hanging pictures, in the dishes drying in the rack and the things left behind, the toothbrushes, the pillows and the coats in the closet.

"So," Mazurski asked, "What furniture we taking?"

"Only one," Skenazy replied. "The drafting table. Leave the rest. If she doesn't want it she can put it on the curb." They disassembled the drafting table. When they left it was almost as if they'd been a pair of strange thieves, stealing nothing of apparent value, leaving things of obvious value, creating minor holes in the fabric of the place —a few dishes, some clothes, some blankets, a poster or a picture frame here or there, a guitar and some amplifiers, records, art supplies, stationery, a shaving kit. When they were finished, Skenazy took one last look, locked the door, tucked the key under the mat, and they departed.

Only for a moment, before they began to unload the cars at the new place, did Skenazy pause to take in his surroundings. "I've always travelled light," he noted, standing on the threshold of the new one-bedroom apartment with the well-walked carpeting. "It never seems like a lot of stuff until you pack it all up and move it and even then… I don't know how I'm gonna fill up these rooms. Maybe I'll just enjoy the space."

"Where you gonna sleep?"

"On an air mattress for now. I'll get my old futon from my mom's this weekend."

They sat on the floor that evening having reassembled the drafting table, the only furniture in the place. They split a 12-pack and ate Chinese food and laughed at the fact that there was nothing in the refrigerator except beer and soy sauce. There was one lamp, and they lit it against the last of the long dusks, and leaned against the wall and let the silence and shadow of Skenazy's new dwelling overtake them.

"I don't think Marjorie was taking advantage of me," Skenazy said, his words floating on the darkness gathering between them. "I think she just doesn't know how to love people. Or maybe she just doesn't know how to love me. She's all wrapped up in herself, I guess. Protected. Afraid. Like she ventured out and then retreated. She was vulnerable, and companionable, only for a little while. I wasn't going to lay siege to her. She'll have to carry on without me." He shrugged. "I guess I'll just lick my wounds and move on. See what comes next."

"You sure moved on today."

"Yeah. Me, my drafting table, my guitar, my *bōgu* and my air mattress. Thanks for helping me out."

*

He had a day off from work, and rather than fill it as he normally would, he set time aside to enjoy it with no fixed plans. Rising late, he bent the spine on a library book over morning coffee in his apartment, Oliver Statler, *Japanese Inn*, and by mid-morning he found he was enjoying the book so much that he decided he'd simply go on reading. It had been years since he'd blown off an entire day to do nothing but read, dismissing other whims, such as calling friends or taking in a movie. He made himself an omelette, holding the book with one hand and the frying pan in the other. Resettling on the couch, he was inspired by the warm sunlight coming through the window to move his operation out of doors. A nearby park held a wide green lawn that sloped down to the bank of a small, swift river, and he had always meant to spend more time there. Armed with an opportunity and a bottle of iced tea, he shrugged into a sweater and set off the few steps.

Reclining on an unoccupied bench in the park, empty except for the occasional dog walker, he fingered the pages until he found his place and resumed his reading. Distracted at first by his circumstances —the novelty of it, the warmth of the day, the hardness of the bench, adjustment of his seat to catch the light through the branches of the trees overhead —he nonetheless slipped somewhat easily back into Statler's world.

Always Armed

He wasn't sure how much of the afternoon slipped away between the turning of the pages but the iced tea was mostly gone when he began to be conscious of the wind in the trees, and with each breath of the wind, the handful of leaves separating from the branches and turning over, spiralling slowly to earth. Every few minutes this happened, and at first he merely appreciated it in passing, but then, as it continued, and more and more leaves began to dot the lawn or the water, he was drawn increasingly to it, found himself waiting for the next time it would happen, became entranced by it —the roaring whisper of the wind and the rustle of the leaves in the branches, the soundless snip of the leaves and their turning plummet. How many years had he seen this phenomenon, he thought, that happens every year in autumn, and yet was seeing it now with new fascination? How had he never been truly present for it before? He recalled very easily —the book was right there on his knee —the samurai's kinship with the cherry blossom. He had never seen Japanese cherry blossoms, but suddenly he appreciated these plain North American leaves in green or yellow or red as he imagined a 17th century swordsman might appreciate the cherry blossoms, with religious reverence, artistic evaluation, and as spiritual contact. He quite forgot the book in his lap, forgot time, as he inhabited the park for the rest of the afternoon watching the infrequent falling of the leaves.

*

He entered the little Episcopal church by a side door and looked around for what he imagined would be a group he was expected to join. But the parishioners taking part in the prayer vigil were not clustered, as if into a squadron; instead they were sprinkled sporadically amidst the pews that extended in diagonal lines from the altar beneath the high ceiling. He took a moment to select a place to sit where he could be seen to be participating, or summoned if that's how it was supposed to work, and yet be by himself. Now what? He had never taken part in a "prayer vigil" before.

But the idea was simple enough. The congregation, at the urging of the pastor, had set aside 24 hours to fill with continuous prayer, and pledged to keep those hours in shifts. Mazurski was one of the people who had chosen this shift, the hour between 2 and 3 o'clock. He wondered who had kept and would be keeping the lonely hours of early morning and late night, what heroes of sacrifice they might be. But no matter. Was he procrastinating? I'm here, Lord, he prayed. I'm just trying to get started. He turned his head over each shoulder and looked around to see if the reverend was present, coaching people, but he was not there.

All right, so let's pray. It's not as if I have to announce myself to you, he thought. You know already why I'm here and what I'm trying to do. But it occurs to me I've never been able to sustain prayer for more than a few minutes. How does one fill an entire hour with it? There were some specific things he and the other parishioners were supposed to pray for —wait a minute, here was the hand-out in his pocket. They were to pray that the church would be a beacon of God's love and fellowship to the area. Yes, he could pray for that. And, in fact, I don't have to put things to you in some format, some holy way, do I? I can just speak my mind to you. I can say, "Hear us O Lord and make unto us a beacon of Thy love to the people around us" or I can just say what I am thinking, which is I wonder what people think of us, if we actually contribute. I wonder what people need. Do I contribute? I guess, God, I can just say I'm glad to be here, and you know what I am asking, but maybe if I try to put it into words it would help not you but me: I'm here with this group of people asking you to help us, make us a better place, make us a community, make us open to the people around us, do good. Maybe I could do better. Are there opportunities I've missed? To be charitable? To be a connection to someone? What must people think of us? Everything's political these days. Do they feel welcome? Am I contributing anything?

In the great silence of the church, a small noise like the scraping of a shoe or a cough broke the quiet but was also pocketed in stillness. Mazurski began to think of other things to pray for, to "do business with God", as the reverend often put it. He could start with gratitude, for his health, for his job, for the privileges he had, and it reminded him to remember others without privileges, and to pray for them, to ask God to lift out of the faceless hordes those that were poor and sick into comfort and safety. A litany of specific people came next to mind, of friends and relatives and then, when he began to remember, he simply let himself remember, and sort of spoke casually to God about these things, about his parents and grandparents and the people in his life, about things he was thinking, about the present and the future. He supposed he could, should, talk to God about the things that were honestly on his mind, and so he allowed himself to pray about kendo, and work, and the movies that interested him, the books he was reading, the little things he was learning about life —he told God about the leaves, added, "But you were there." He thought, too, of women, and this lead him to think of sin, not the sins of lust but of the various failings in his relationships, the pains he'd inflicted and that had been inflicted on him, the sorrows and regrets. And the hopes. And he remembered, too, that the reverend had reminded them they could "be still and know that I am God," so when he ran out of things to say he just let them run out until something else occurred to him. If you were here, he thought, with me, like a mortal person, we would be able to sit side by side without speaking, like, I dunno, two guys fishing.

As he struggled to remember, to be relevant, to pray, to be still, he began to think that perhaps this prayer vigil was of just as much benefit to him as to God and "spiritual warfare." He was contributing to something metaphysical, he was sure. But he was also simply practicing discipline. And then it occurred to him —he knew something about discipline. Because of kendo, he was a disciplined person. He knew what discipline meant, it meant to consistently practise and apply what one practised. Perhaps kendo could inform, had informed, his spiritual life. Perhaps showing up for church, and taking part in a prayer vigil, and the constant, casual study and application of what he studied in his every day walk of life, was just like kendo. One "practised" his faith, as one practised kendo, was part of a community that met in a special place each week to work at it with a teacher or teachers. One was a "disciple" because he was "disciplined". One applied what he learned. Had his kendo life become like church? Could his church life be more like kendo?

He glanced at his watch. Still a quarter of an hour to go. He asked God, what do you think of my idea?

*

As the obnoxious guy at the party grinned and teased, the karate student developed a sly smile and leaned a bit closer. The act of leaning caused a shift in the atmosphere of the little, drunken conversation toward a sudden tension, despite the fact that the karate man smiled and spoke jovially.

"Hey, man, you're right. You don't have to tell me! But check it out, you say you have a shotgun that can tear me to pieces? I don't doubt it. But where is that shotgun now? Right now?"

The karate man let that word hang there for a moment. He brought a hand up in a gesture that was meant to wave dismissively at the air between them but which, Mazurski now saw, everyone saw, could also have escalated into an attack with little change. "See, your weapon isn't on you, is it? Your weapon is at home in a closet somewhere? Right? Am I right?" The karate man laughed and leaned closer, making a point with fingers that were now inches away from the antagonist's chest. "But my weapon? Well…" he balled his hand into a fist and moved it closer. "My weapon is always on me. You have a weapon that can tear me to pieces. But you don't have your weapon with you. I have mine with me. I can get to my weapon and you can't get to yours."

The karate student was leaning very close to the obnoxious man, now, and his smile was tight. The obnoxious man was startled enough, realised or seemed to realise that he was now in an imminent fist fight, that he said nothing, only looked apprehensive, looked for a place to set his beer down, leaned away as the karate student leaned in.

Suddenly the karate student burst into a smile, brushed the obnoxious man gently on the shoulder, and said, "I'm just messing with you!" He burst into laughter. The other people in the circle, including Mazurski, chuckled nervously. "Good one," said the obnoxious man, wagging a finger, relieved, but also finding new reservoirs of anger, someone who had obviously been one-upped and wasn't yet sure what he was going to do about it. Happily, a girlfriend of his took him by the elbow and led him away, and the karate student began to gravitate in another direction to give him space. The karate student said to Mazurski, "What an ass, eh? I suppose I shouldn't have said anything."

"I don't know, man, that was pretty cool," Mazurski admitted.

"No, I risked escalating it."

"Well, you could have handled it." For whatever reason, Mazurski felt a need to add something self-denigrating, to take himself out of the same category as the karate man. "Hey, I might be okay in a sword fight but otherwise I'm useless."

Reaching for another couple of beers, the karate student looked at Mazurski with eyes serious and a mouth amused. "Don't kid me, man," he said. "You, too, are always armed." He placed the lip of the beer bottle's cap on the edge of the table and with one smooth thrust of the palm popped it open and handed it to Mazurski.

Peer Reviewed

Sports-related injuries in Kendo
—a systematic review of the medical literature—

Darryl C. Tong BDS, MBChB, MSD, FFDRCSI, FDSRCS, FACOMS, Sir John Walsh Research Institute, University of Otago, Dunedin, New Zealand

Alex Bennett MA, PhD (Canterbury), PhD (Kyoto), Kansai University, Osaka, Japan

Abstract

Aims: To systematically summarise the scientific literature looking at injuries sustained in kendo and to highlight the need for longitudinal data collection.

Method: A systematic review of the scientific medical literature was conducted using web-based online and manual hard-copy searches of articles relevant to sports-related injuries in kendo. A simple set of inclusion criteria was used to identify articles suitable for systematic review. Editorials, opinion letters, kinesiology studies, and sports performance enhancement studies were excluded.

Results: From 82 potentially relevant articles screened, 17 articles met the simple inclusion criteria. There were no randomised controlled trials and all but one of the articles included for review were case reports or case series, the exception being a cross-sectional prevalence study. The majority of injuries sustained in kendo were musculoskeletal followed by haemoglobinuria issues in female kendo practitioners. The incidence and range of injuries in kendo cannot be commented on due to a lack of data, but compared to other martial arts such as taekwondo and aikido, they appear to be low in number and minor in severity.

Conclusions: Exertion and repetitive impact forces appear to be the major factors in the injuries seen in kendo. The relatively small numbers of published articles relating to sports-related kendo injuries may not accurately reflect the true incidence and further research is recommended.

Key Words: *kendo, martial arts, sports injuries*

Introduction

The practice of budo combines physical, mental and spiritual training and development. Although all of the traditional forms of budo were historically practised for self-defence or combat purposes, some forms emphasise the self-development and health aspect rather than the martial aspect of the art, in particular *tai chi* where the slow rhythmic movements involving balance and breathing may be particularly beneficial for older people.[1-3] In a comparative study of injuries in martial arts, head/neck, groin and upper and lower extremity injuries were more common in taekwondo and head/neck, upper extremity and soft tissue injuries were more common in aikido.[4] The injury rate in taekwondo was 59% and 51% in aikido compared to 30% in karate with people over the age of 18 showing a statistically significant increased risk of being injured than those under the age of 18 years of age.

In another study of martial arts injuries, a U.S.-based five year national survey showed that almost three quarters of martial arts injuries involved the extremities and 95% of all injuries were mild to moderate in nature not requiring hospitalization.[5] Apart from musculoskeletal injuries, concussion and sub-concussive injuries are also prevalent in martial arts. Chronic traumatic brain injury (CBTI) from repetitive concussion is well described in boxing but has also been identified in other contact sports such as American football, soccer, ice hockey and in martial arts such as karate and taekwondo.[6,7] In particular with taekwondo, the head is a legitimate target for kicks and one paper reported 1009 head blows identified on video analysis during a single ten-day tournament. The single most frequent anatomical site for head blows in taekwondo was the temporal region.[7] More sinister consequences may arise from traumatic brain injury sustained in training and competition, as reported in the *Japan Times*,[31] with revelations that over one hundred deaths among students aged between 12 to 17 as a result of judo accidents in Japanese schools occurred over a 27-year period (1983 to 2009) - an average of four deaths a year, giving an incidence five times higher than in any other sport. About 65 per cent of these fatalities were associated with brain injuries and the article suggested that a "dangerous trend" existed among Japanese schools. Nakiri et al. studied the impact forces transmitted through kendo protective hear gear during *men* and *tsuki* strikes using accelerometers in both human and simulation subjects to determine its safety.[8] Findings from this study showed that although a single impact to the head is not serious enough to cause cranial bone or concussive injuries, long term repetitive strikes to the head could potentially lead to chronic subdural haematoma formation. Further research into this area was recommended. Whereas there are studies reporting on the incidence and patterns of injury related to other martial arts such as karate and taekwondo, little is written about injuries specific to the practice of kendo. The aim of this review is to systematically summarise the medical literature looking at injuries sustained in kendo, with the specific research question to be addressed: *What is the most common sports-related injury in kendo?*

Methods

Search strategy

Web-based online databases (PubMed, ISI Web of Science, Medscape and Google Scholar), the Cochrane Library and hand-searches of major journals, reference texts and published abstracts were used to perform a literature review. For web-based online searches the following key words were used to identify relevant publications: "kendo" OR "kendo injuries" OR "kendo sports injuries". The abstract of each article was reviewed and the relevant articles retrieved for further evaluation including a further literature search utilizing the reference list from the publications themselves. Information about the reported injuries or conditions was collated and summarised for discussion.

Article evaluation

Articles identified by online and hand searches were evaluated using a set of inclusion and exclusion criteria. Articles fulfilling all inclusion criteria were accepted for review. The criteria for including studies were:

* Literature reporting on sports injuries related to kendo
* Literature reporting on medical conditions related to kendo practice

Study Design

In terms of study design, the articles sought were randomized controlled trials (RCTs); prospective or retrospective cohort studies; review articles, case controlled studies and case reports. Some studies not specifically related to kendo injuries were considered for reference. Editorials and opinion pieces were not accepted for review. Publications limited to scientific literature and reference texts were included for review.

Critical appraisal of the articles

Studies that did not fulfil the simple inclusion criteria were excluded, however, further reasons for not accepting publications for final analysis included kinesiology studies; studies investigating metabolic and biochemical markers, and sports performance or enhancement studies.

Statistical analysis
No statistical analysis was performed due to the heterogeneity of the data reported and the limited numbers of participants in case series.

Results
Study inclusion and exclusion
Figure 1 summarises the search strategy used to make the final selection of publications for review. Using PubMed, "kendo" yielded 74 results; "kendo injuries" yielded 15 results and "kendo sports injuries" yielded 12 results. A combined search using all the terms yielded 12 results. Using ISI Web of Science, "kendo" yielded 94 results; "kendo injuries" yielded 16 results; "kendo sports injuries" yielded seven results and the combined search yielded seven results. Using Medscape, "kendo sports injuries" yielded 309 results but "kendo" and "kendo injuries" yielded no results. The combined search yielded no results.

Using Google Scholar, "kendo" yielded 7,930 results; "kendo injuries" yielded 1,250 results and "kendo sports injuries" yielded 646 results. A combined search using all these terms yielded 366 results.

After the removal of duplicate search results and using a manual search, a total of 82 articles were included for initial review. Subsequent evaluation of these articles however removed a further 65 articles due to not meeting the inclusion criteria fully, or the data was not clearly kendo related. This gave a final total of 18 articles that met the inclusion criteria for this review.[9–26]

Study characteristics
Of the 18 articles selected for final review, 13 were case reports, four were case series and one was a cross-sectional prevalence study. There were no RCTs, prospective or retrospective cohort studies. Seven articles described musculoskeletal injuries; five articles described "medical" conditions including a case report of frictional dermatitis and three articles described injuries to the aerodigestive tract. The remaining two articles involved vascular abnormalities. Table 1 summarises some of the major characteristics of the papers included for review.

Musculoskeletal injuries
Four articles described lower limb injuries involving the initial diagnosis of stress fractures of the foot or the medial malleolus.[14,15,17,18] In one of the case reports, the aetiology of the foot pain was found to be related to an osteoid osteoma formation of the metatarsal rather than a stress fracture. The mechanism of injury was believed to be from repetitive impact force on the lower extremities on hard surfaces.

There was one case report for each of the following: bilateral stress fractures of the ulnae,[19] stress fracture of the ulnar styloid process,[20] and avascular necrosis of the lunate and scaphoid bones in a 67 year-old female kendo practitioner.[25] Unlike the injuries to the foot and ankle, these injuries were due to being repetitively struck on the wrist from *kote* strikes.

The one cross-sectional prevalence study included for review was a comparative study of lumbar intervertebral disc degeneration in athletes involved in baseball, basketball, soccer, running, swimming and kendo.[23]

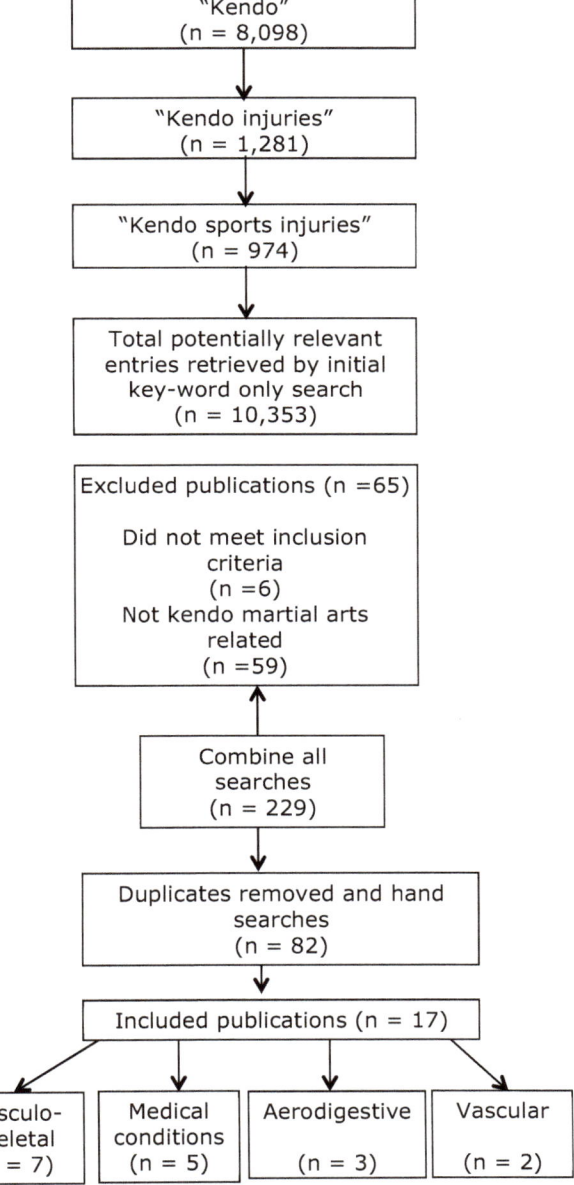

Figure 1. Search strategy flowchart summary

References	Study Design	Sample size	Injury reported	Commentary
Asai et al. (1986)	Case series	3	March haemoglobinuria	Haemoglobinuria in female kendoka due to exertion during practice
Hangai et al. (2009)	Cross sectional prevalence study	308	Lumbar intervertebral disc degeneration	Prevalence study of lumbar disc degeneration over several sporting codes including kendo. 84% of kendoka reported lower back pain during their lifetime.
Hara et al. (2009)	Case report	1	Oesophageal dissecting haematoma	Description of oesophageal pain in a 69-year old kendoka on low dose aspirin.
Inoue et al. (2004)	Case report	1	Haemoptysis	15-year-old kendoka with three month history of haemoptysis due to pulmonary thromboembolism from subclavian vein injury
Ishimoto et al. (2003)	Case report	1	Aneurysm of dorsal superficial antebrachial artery right wrist	Pseudoaneurysm of anomaly of radial artery in right wrist following repetitive *kote* strikes
Itadera et al. (2001)	Case report	1	Stress fracture of ulnar styloid process	Stress fracture in left wrist due to flexing towards ulnar direction during striking
Iwasaki et al. (2010)	Case report	1	Bilateral wrist injuries	Avascular necrosis of lunate bone of right wrist and scaphoid bone of left wrist in a 67-year old kendoka sustained from repetitive *kote* strikes
Komatsu et al. (1992)	Case report	1	Pneumomediastinum	Pneumomediastinum caused by closed tracheal injury due to blunt force trauma from *tsuki*.
Mineoka et al. (1984)	Case report	1	March haemoglobinuria	Haemoglobinuria in a female kendoka following exertion
Nakatsuji et al. (1978)	Case series	2	March haemoglobinuria	Haemoglobinuria in two female kendoka following exertion during rigorous practice
Nunn et al. (1997)	Case series	5	Plantar fasciitis of the right foot	Four out of five women kendoka in the British National Kendo Squad had plantar fasciitis. Measurements of foot impact showed a mean force of four times body weight during *fumikomi*. The quality of training floors and possibly a change in footwork was highlighted.
Okada et al. (1995)	Case series	2	Stress fractures of medial malleolus	Minor stress fractures of the right medial malleolus attributed to repetitive *fumikomi*
Sakai et al. (1986)	Case report	1	Carotid aneurysm	Non-fatal dissecting carotid aneurysm attributed to constant frictional trauma from kendo protective headgear
Sakamoto et al. (1989)	Case report	1	Osteoid osteoma of 5th metatarsal left foot	Unusual presentation of osteoid osteoma of 5th metatarsal attributed to *fumikomi*
Sujino et al. (1997)	Case report	1	Bilateral stress fractures of the ulnae	Bilateral stress fractures of the ulnae in a beginner kendoka following rigorous striking at a training camp
Urabe et al. (1986)	Case report	1	March haemoglobinuria	Haemoglobinuria in a female kendoka following exertion
Yokoe and Mannoji (1986)	Case series	3	Stress fractures of proximal phalanx of the great toe	Stress fractures of the great toe reported in three kendoka attributed to *fumikomi*
Yoshida et al. (2010)	Case report	1	Hyperkeratosis and frictional dermatitis of foot	Painful hyperkeratosis of the right heel and skin changes on the sole of the left foot due to kendo footwork

Table 1. Summary of characteristics of articles selected for review

Aerodigestive tract injuries

Three articles described injuries or abnormalities involving the oesophagus or respiratory system. There was one case report of a dissecting intramural haematoma of the oesophagus causing pain, vomiting and dysphagia in a 69-year-old man on low-dose aspirin.[24] Another case report described a 15-year-old with a three month history of haemoptysis [22] and the remaining article reported the potentially life-threatening injury of pneumomediastinum as a result from blunt force trauma to the larynx.[16]

Vascular injuries

Two case reports involved abnormalities of vascular structures; one report described a vascular injury localised to the wrist resulting in an aneurysm of the dorsal superficial antebrachial artery [21] (Ishimoto et al. 2003) and the other report involved a life-threatening dissecting aneurysm of the carotid artery due to repetitive frictional rubbing from protective headgear (Sakai et al. 1986).[12]

"Medical" conditions

The remaining five articles described conditions that were not overtly associated with external injury or impact force.

Four articles described march haemoglobinuria in female kendo practitioners [9-11,13] and one case report of painful hyperkeratosis and frictional dermatitis affecting the heel of the right foot [26] attributed to repetitive mechanical trauma to the soles of the feet due to kendo footwork.

Discussion

Kendo is a traditional form of budo that has origins in combat swordsmanship developed by samurai during feudal times.[27,28] After the Second World War, all martial arts were banned in Japan by the Occupation Forces, but some of these forms were modified in such a way as to minimise the martial aspects and emphasise the physical training and spiritual development aspects instead. Shedding itself of the pre-war stigma of militarism and ultra-nationalism, kendo was re-established nearly a decade after Japan's wartime defeat as a "democratic sport". Emphasis was placed on the competitive aspects, and later on this was balanced with rhetoric stressing its educational and traditional values.

Protective body armour is used, allowing the kendo practitioner (kendoka) to freely strike target areas with a split bamboo sword, mimicking the use of a real sword to inflict lethal or incapacitating blows to the opponent. These target areas are shown in Figure 2. Significant sports injuries are not commonly associated with kendo when compared to other martial arts such as taekwondo, karate, aikido, and judo, perhaps in part due to limiting strikes to protected areas, but also due to the absence of throws, flips or kicks in kendo training. Nonetheless, kendo movements can be both explosive and violent in nature, especially in striking the opponent.

It is difficult to determine the true incidence of kendo-related sports injuries given the relative scarcity of scientific literature, and that no randomised control trials or any clinical trials have been published. The scientific strength of the majority of the publications identified for review is poor, with 16 of the 17 articles being a case report or a case series, describing clinical observations or oddities. The one cross-sectional prevalence study reviewed involved kendo as part of a comparison group with other sports looking at lumbar intervertebral disc degeneration in athletes.[23] In this study, self-reported lower back pain was compared in a number of competitive sports activities (baseball, swimming, basketball, kendo, soccer and running) against non-athletes among 19- to 20-year-old students at a university in Japan. Of the 51 kendo practitioners who participated in this study, 84% reported lower back pain during their lifetime and 21% within the last four weeks of completing the questionnaire. It is unclear whether or not the questionnaire limited the lower back pain only to sports related activities however. Over 40% of the participants reported moderate to severe lower back pain

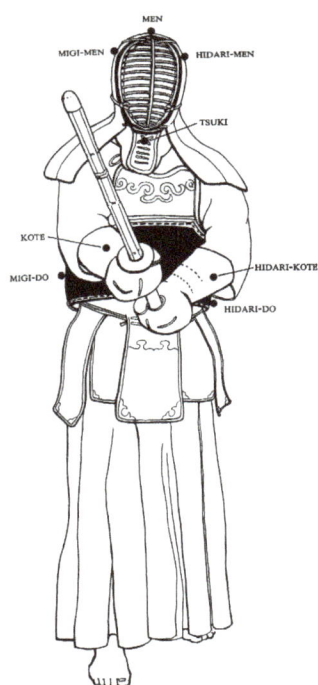

Figure 2. Target strike zones in kendo

Adapted from Sasamori J, Warner G. *This is Kendo—The Art of Japanese Fencing*. Rutland, VT: Charles E. Tuttle Company Publishers 1992:76.

and one quarter reported radiating leg symptoms. Baseball and swimming activities were among the highest for lower back pain and the study concluded that lower back pain may be a predictor of disc degeneration in young athletes due to the various movements and postures associated with each sport. This would appear consistent with anecdotal accounts that back pain is common in kendo which is usually attributed to poor posture.

Among the case reports, the most common injuries were musculoskeletal in nature and involved the extremities. This is consistent with findings from a national survey in the United States looking at all martial arts injuries over a five-year period.[15]

Avascular necrosis of the lunate and scaphoid bones (Kienbock's and Preiser's disease, respectively) was reported in an elderly female kendoka with the mechanism of injury attributed to minor, repetitive trauma to the wrist. This would be entirely consistent with repetitive strikes to the wrist and the authors wished to raise awareness of these boney degenerative diseases as potential sports related problems in elderly kendo practitioners.[25]

Repetitive trauma may not only be due to being struck by the opponent but may also be associated with the explosive movements of the kendoka themselves as they perform a strike. A difficult movement for beginners (and some more advanced) is the coordination of striking the target and stomping the forward (right) foot at time of impact - *fumikomi-ashi*.[29,30] This type of stomping action can generate significant impact forces and according to research conducted by the All Japan Kendo Federation, a male kendoka generates an average force of 884.6 kg in the vertically downward direction of his right foot when striking the men or approximately thirteen times their average body weight.[29]

Nunn et al.[18] reported repetitive strain foot injuries in four high-level competitive women kendoka, recording their impact forces during training. According to this case series, these elite women kendoka performed *fumikomi-ashi* approximately every 15–20 seconds during training with the right foot impacting against the floor up to 200 times during a one-hour practice. Foot impact vertical forces reached up to 4000N in one of the subjects and 3500N in two other subjects (approximately four times body weight) highlighting the need to select appropriate flooring for kendo training in order to prevent foot or ankle injuries.

General exertion during training due to repetitive strikes, rigorous footwork and shouting (*kiai*) may also lead to injuries or conditions not directly related to being struck by the opponent. A case report of an otherwise healthy 15-year-old with a three-month history of haemoptysis revealed a subclavian vein thrombosis leading to pulmonary thromboembolism.[22] The subclavian thrombosis was attributed to a combination of rigorous arm swings and a hypercoagulable state induced by dehydration. Similarly, a 69-year-old man on low dose aspirin developed a dissecting intramural haematoma of the oesophagus causing pain, vomiting and dysphagia as a result of kendo training, a warning perhaps that older kendoka on cardio-protective anticoagulants should seek medical advice or at least be warned of potential complications related to the medication and strenuous physical activity.[24] Hard training may also lead to march haemoglobinuria (blood in the urine from exertion), which was reported four times as individual case reports or case series in female kendoka.[9-11,13] The two most significant and imminently life threatening injuries include blunt trauma mechanisms, one involving a dissecting aneurysm of the carotid as a result of rubbing from the *men* and the other involving a closed tracheal injury causing late pneumomediastinum in a 17-year-old male.[12,16] The carotid aneurysm was a result of a rare incident whereas the tracheal injury resulted from a direct thrust to the throat with the tip of the bamboo sword used by advanced kendoka. Although the midline neck is protected by a thick leather flange, this technique is not encouraged in junior or beginner kendoka and is generally prohibited against children and older individuals in fighting and practice.

There were no reports of Achilles tendon injury and other tendon injuries such as lateral epicondylitis (tennis elbow or in this case "kendo" elbow) in the scientific literature although anecdotally these appear to be very common injuries. Perhaps due to the minor nature of the injury or its common occurrence, no formal study has been published although several kendo websites discuss these injuries. Lower extremity injuries ranging from minor sprains and toenail injuries to major dislocations and tendon rupture are more common in kendo than upper extremity injuries and head injuries.[30]

The question of what is the most common sports-related injury in kendo can only be partly addressed by this review due to the limitations of published literature. Most of the injuries identified from the published medical literature appear to be musculoskeletal and minor in nature but the true incidence and patterns of injury is not known, and may differ from country to country influenced by factors such as age of participants, physical build and perhaps more pertinent, how kendo is taught and practised, and the training environment. This includes factors such as climate, but most importantly, as kendo is practised in bare feet, the shock-absorbent qualities or hardness of the floor.

Conclusion and Recommendations

From this systematic review it would appear that being struck repetitively and constant exertion during training are common factors associated with kendo-related sports injuries, with the musculoskeletal system the most commonly involved. However, due to the small number of publications and the anecdotal nature of the papers reviewed, further research is needed in order to identify patterns of injury and true incidence in terms of primary data collection and open reporting of injuries sustained during practice. Perhaps a starting point would be to establish a database for longitudinal data collection in each of the major kendo federations with details including age, height, weight, experience level in kendo, how the injury was sustained, type and severity of injury, interventions, and outcomes. This level of detail would give a clearer indication of sports-related injuries in kendo; however the data collected must still be presented at a national organisation level in order for monitoring and changes in training curricula to be made in terms of safety and best practice. The safety of our young practitioners must be a priority to ensure a successful continuity for the future of budo.

Acknowledgements

The authors wish to thank Dr Masakazu Niimi DDS, PhD for his assistance with Japanese translation in the preparation of this manuscript.

References

1. Wang C, Collet JP, Lau J. "The effect of Tai Chi on health outcomes in patients with chronic conditions: a systematic review". Arch Int Med 30:2039-2044, 2004.
2. Burke DT, Al-Adawi S, Lee YT, Audette J. "Martial arts as sport and therapy". J Sports Med Phys Fitness 47:96-102, 2007.
3. Bu B, Haijun H, Yong L et al. "Effects of martial arts on health status: A systematic review". JEBM 3:205-219, 2010.
4. Zetaruk MN, Violan MA, Zurakowski D, Micheli LJ. "Injuries in martial arts: a comparison of five styles". Br J Sports Med 39:29-33, 2005.
5. Birrer RB, Halbrook SP. "Martial arts injuries: The results of a five year national survey". Am J Sports Med 16:408-410, 1988.
6. Rabadi MH, Jordan BD. "The cumulative effect of repetitive concussion in sports". Clin J Sport Med 11: 194-198, 2001.
7. Koh JA, Watkinson EJ, Yoon YJ. "Video analysis of head blows leading to concussion in competition taekwondo". Brain Injury 18: 1287-1296, 2004.
8. Nakiri F, Yokoyama N, Arita Y, Kubo T, Yamagami S. "Influence of Datotsu in kendo on the human head: impact estimation using simulation with crash dummy". Research Journal of Budo 37: 1-11, 2005.
9. Nakatsuji T, Oda S, Fujita H et al. "So called march hemoglobinuria caused by kendo exercise: a report of two cases". Rinsho Ketsueki 19:1241-1246, 1978.
10. Mineoka K, Yamamoto K, Isemura T et al. "A case of march hemoglobinuria following kendo (Japanese fencing) exercise". Rinsho Ketsueki 25:1680-1685, 1984.
11. Asai T, Itoh K, Oh H et al. "March hemoglobinuria caused by kendo: report on 3 cases with exertion test of kendo and study on erythrocyte membrane SDS-PAGE". Rinsho Ketsueki 27:179-184, 1986.
12. Sakai H, Kaneko D, Yuki K et al. "Carotid dissecting aneurysm due to blunt (rubbing) injury of the kendo protector". No Shinkei Geka 14:91-94, 1986.
13. Urabe M, Hara Y, Hokama A et al. "A female case of march hemoglobinuria induced by kendo (Japanese fencing) exercise". Nippon Niaka Gakkai Zasshi 75:1657-1658, 1986.
14. Yokoe K, Mannoji T. "Stress fracture of the proximal phalanx of the great toe. A report of three cases". Am J of Sports Med 14: 240-242, 1986.
15. Sakamoto K, Mizuta H, Okajima K et al. "An unusual case of metatarsal pain in a young kendo player". Am J Sports Med 17:296-297, 1989.
16. Komatsu H, Enzan K, Mitsuhara H et al. "A case of pneumomediastinum caused by closed tracheal injury during the game of kendo (Japanese fencing)". Masui 41:673-676, 1992.
17. Okada K, Senma S, Abe E et al. "Stress fractures of the medial malleolus: a case report". Foot Ankle Int 16:49-52, 1995.
18. Nunn NR, Dyas JW, Dodd IP. "Repetitive strain injury to the foot in elite women kendoka". Br J Sports Med 31:68-69, 1997.
19. Sujino T, Ohe T, Shinozuka M. "Bilateral stress fractures of the ulnae in a kendo (Japanese fencing) player". Br J Sports Med 32:340-342, 1998.
20. Itadera E, Ichikawa N, Hashizume H et al. "Stress fracture of the ulnar styloid process in kendo player- a case report". Hand Surg 6:109-111, 2001.
21. Ishimoto T, Shindo S, Satoshi N et al. "Aneurysm formation of a dorsal superficial antebrachial artery due to sports injury. A case report". Vasc Endovasc Surg 37:141-143, 2003.
22. Inoue K, Saito J, Miyazaki M et al. "A kendo player with haemoptysis". Lancet 364:814, 2004.
23. Hangai M, Kaneoka K, Hinotsu S et al. "Lumbar intervertebral disk degeneration in athletes". Am J Sports Med 37:149-155, 2009.
24. Hara H, Sakai E, Inokuchi Y et al. "Dissecting intramural hematoma of the esophagus in a kendo player taking low-dose aspirin". Inter Med 48:2153-2154, 2009.
25. Iwasaki N, Masuko T, Funakoshi T et al. "Elderly kendo (Japanese fencing) player with Kienbock's disease in one wrist and Preiser's disease in the other wrist: a case report". Hand Surg 15:47-51, 2010.
26. Yoshida M, Oiso N, Kawada A. "Hyperkeratosis and frictional dermatitis from practicing kendo". Case Rep Dermatol 2:65-68, 2010.
27. Sasamori J, Warner G. *This is Kendo—The Art of Japanese Fencing*. Rutland, VT: Charles E. Tuttle Company Publishers, p76, 1992.
28. Donahue JJ. *Complete Kendo*. Boston: Tuttle Publishing, pp1-5, 1999.
29. Ozawa H. *Kendo: The Definitive Guide*. Tokyo: Kodansha International, pp132-133, 1997.
30. Tokeshi J. *Kendo: Elements, Rules and Philosophy*. Honolulu: University of Hawaii Press, pp207-212, 2003.
31. Japan Times, "108 school judo class deaths but no charges, only silence", August 26, 2010

craftmanship worthy of praise

"Every Kote I make is something Special"
— Kazuki Unzei, Bogu Craftsman

TOZANDO

www.tozandoshop.com

Kendo Kote Workshop
- Custom-made *kote* worth wearing

The Tozando Kendo Kote Workshop is based in Iwate prefecture, Japan. The master craftsmen working there take pride in producing 100% Japan-made *kote* of the highest possible quality.

We at Tozando felt that it was time to take things to the next level. In 2014, we established the Kendo Kote Workshop website (*www.kendokote.com*). For the first time ever, we revealed all of our accumulated experience and craftsmanship to customers around the world.

One of the master craftsmen at the Kendo Kote Workshop is Mr. Kazuki Unzei, who works at our Nishijin store in Kyoto. We asked him what's so different about the Tozando Kendo Kote Workshop and also about his aspirations as a craftsman:

"The Kendo Kote Workshop offers unique products, completely custom-made to the purchaser's specifications. That is what makes our products different from anything else available on the market. As a craftsman, every kote I make is something special, and I hope that the customer will use it with love and care for years to come.

I am blessed with a master who is willing to teach me, and pass down his knowledge to me. Although I still have much left to learn from my teacher, my goal is to make the ultimate bogu someday..."

Our kendo *kote* are made according to the traditional protocols for *bogu* manufacture. Our craftsmen pour their heart and souls into their work, and we have confidence that you will see the difference. We are the one and only Kendo Kote Workshop.

Tozando Co., Ltd.
www.tozando.com

www.kendokote.com